M000305468

GROW AND SELL
YOUR START-UP

GROW AND SELL YOUR START-UP

How to create a business you can sell for millions

FIONA HUDSON-KELLY

Grow and Sell Your Start-up

ISBN 978-1-915483-04-1
eISBN 978-1-915483-05-8

Published in 2023 by Right Book Press

© Fiona Hudson-Kelly 2023

The right of Fiona Hudson-Kelly to be identified as the author of this work has been asserted in accordance with the Copyright, Designs and Patents Act 1988.

A CIP record of this book is available from the British Library.

All rights reserved. No part of this book may be reproduced, stored in a retrieval system, or transmitted in any form or by any means, electronic, mechanical, photocopying, recording or otherwise, without the prior written permission of the copyright holder.

Contents

Introduction

When you're an entrepreneur with a passion for business, you know the power of big dreams. So imagine, one day in a few years' time, waking up to see tens of millions in your bank account. And to know that it's from the sale of your company to a buyer whom you trust to take good care of it *and* who doesn't insist on you staying to run it. Welcome to a new kind of freedom.

If that sounds like the sort of thing that's only for Silicon Valley start-ups, I'm here to tell you otherwise. I created my most recent business, Smart Apprentices, when I was a single mum financing four children through school, with very little to support me. And yet ten years later I sold it, exiting with the sort of payout above. I was also able to walk away from the company rather than being obliged to stay on at the helm, which gave me the ability to pursue other ambitions.

I'm not special. I didn't go to university or come from an entrepreneurial background; nor am I a techie or a finance expert. In fact, when I set up the first of my four businesses, I didn't know anyone who'd done the same thing. I've learned about entrepreneurship the hard way – through making mistakes, learning from them and lots of hard work. What I'm sharing with you in this book is how to start, scale and sell your own business so that you can achieve the exit you want – the one that's right for you. Even if perhaps you don't think it's possible.

Smart Apprentices is my fourth business. My first, launched when I was in my 20s, grew rapidly into a successful training company but eventually crashed and burned. The second attracted several million pounds of investment from backers but didn't give me the satisfaction I wanted (although it was sold for millions). And the third was vulnerable at times but ultimately came good.

I often think that if I'd been able to do my fourth business first, I would have saved myself a lot of problems. Unfortunately time travel still isn't possible, despite advances in technology. This book is therefore the one I wish I'd had to guide me right from the beginning. If I'd known what (and what not) to do all along, I wonder what I could have achieved and how quickly it would have happened. Not that I'm unhappy with where I am now; I've just turned 60 and am looking forward to spending the rest of my life doing what I want. But it could have been so much smoother if I'd known how to start, scale and sell when I first began my entrepreneurial journey.

How I did it

My childhood in the 1960s and 70s was not an easy one, although it didn't always seem hard to me at the time. Both my parents were dysfunctional and we had little money, so I took care of my younger siblings as best I could. While in many ways I regret the difficulties I had to deal with, they did teach me about independence. I knew that, if I didn't want my life to be like my mum's, I had to work out how to make it different. I saw that being dealt a bad hand in life didn't mean that I couldn't create the one I wanted in the future, and it never occurred to me to think that anyone but myself was going to do that for me.

After I left school with few qualifications, I landed an apprenticeship at Rolls-Royce, a major manufacturer in my area, and found myself with both money and independence for the first time. Learning in a practical way was what I loved most, and thanks to the support I had from two female role models in the business, Norma and Peta, I progressed to being responsible for the company's entire trainee and apprentice cohorts.

When the plant closed, I took redundancy and started working as a college lecturer. I enjoyed the job and saw that developments within colleges were getting interesting; they were starting to create commercial courses for organisations that needed to use computers. When I was asked to cover some of the teaching for this, I was astonished at how much the colleges were charging for generic group sessions. I figured that, if companies were willing to pay that much for a basic product, there must be a gap in the market for more personalised training programmes.

So without doing any market research or even thinking much about it, I set up my first business on the side. With the help of Dianne, one of my brightest students, I opened an office with a single computer. I called it Start-Right Computer Training, which was apt because it truly was the start of my entrepreneurial journey.

Right start, fast start

After a slow beginning, I managed to land a meeting with the training director at Peugeot. Dianne and I created a bespoke Microsoft Excel course for his sales director, which he loved, and more people from the company then signed up. We'd swot up on the material by reading books about it the night before, and hey presto by morning we were experts in it. Eventually my college employers gave me an ultimatum: run my business or keep my job with them. I took the plunge and went into Start-Right full time.

'What on earth do you think you're doing?' said my husband, family and friends. 'You're leaving your job and setting up a company? Don't be ridiculous. People like you don't do that.' About the last bit they were right – I knew nobody who owned a company, let alone another woman. But I wanted to be independent and make my own decisions in life.

Over the next few years, through a combination of determination and a laser focus on the customer experience, I grew Start-Right into a booming business. Even though I didn't have a dedicated salesperson, I managed to add three or four huge automotive company clients to my roster. When people ask me how we grew so rapidly I say it's because we looked after our clients incredibly well, recruiting others on the back of recommendations we gained. And of course there was my business model. Instead of trying to compete with large, national trainers who laid on blanket group courses at their own offices, we offered bespoke, private sessions that were tailored to our clients' needs.

This led to us winning awards and, over time, adding another 45 employees to the payroll. We recruited people who were young and enthusiastic and trained them up in-house; as long as they were bright and ready to contribute to our energetic, fun company culture, they could be part of our team. We all enjoyed the Friday pizza nights, when my kids would come in and play computer games with the staff. It was a lovely atmosphere. Getting the culture right, and recruiting and training the best people, was one of the things that we did well.

However, I was blind to the fault lines that were running through my business. We didn't charge enough, we were financially naive and we didn't have any sales and marketing skills in-house – that's why we only had four clients, albeit large ones. I also had no senior leadership team and ran around doing all the administration myself. It was no way to run a business.

More seriously, I didn't have a strategy or exit plan. Why would I? I was able to pay myself well, which meant I could buy a nice house, put my children through private school and hire nannies. We were well respected as a training provider, and because of the household names we had as customers, I just assumed we would go on forever. If I'd taken a step back and looked at the macro environment I was operating within, I'd have foreseen the rise of competitors to the UK manufacturing industry arriving from the rest of Europe and the Far East, ready to challenge British inefficiencies. This made our clients vulnerable.

Other things were changing as well: in the mid-80s computers were becoming easier to use, and then Microsoft's Windows arrived, which was more intuitive than what had been available before. This reduced the need for companies to train their staff when they started a new job. Hot on the heels of that the Internet arrived, leading to more courses being delivered online. Because I didn't foresee all this I couldn't insulate the business against it, which meant that I didn't see the end coming.

One customer at a time, it all came tumbling down. Peugeot was the first to bow out when it closed its facility in Coventry, and we lost all the others, including the Rover Group, over the next year. Our financial situation was made worse by the fact that we'd tripled the size of our facilities six months previously. We'd planned to add financial services customers to our roster of manufacturing clients, but it hadn't occurred to us to research how viable this would be. I'm convinced that if we'd diversified our client base earlier, we might have struggled through the demise of Rover. But because we'd invested so heavily in offices and were dependent on a narrow customer base, Start-Right was soon to be no more. Although, to give me my due, it was really, really successful while it lasted – 17 years is way longer than most small firms survive.

Towards the end, not only did my business collapse

but my marriage also broke down – it was a horrendous time. By now I had four children, with my youngest only a few months old. Although I wasn't saddled by much business debt and had managed to close Start-Right without owing money to suppliers, I'd signed a personal guarantee on the lease of our new office building. I had to sell my house to pay for it, which meant moving my young family into rented accommodation. I was in shock. How had it gone wrong so quickly? What was I going to do? One thing was sure, I had to get back on my feet without delay.

A silver lining appears

I had no house or assets, so my options seemed limited. That's when I asked myself the question every entre-preneur starts with: 'What's the opportunity?' I had expertise in training and technology so I employed one of my Start-Right trainers, who was also a computer programmer, to write a clever piece of software. It was a skills assessment programme for businesses to find out how much their people knew about a subject (we'd call it a quiz now). I had the idea because I remembered how tricky it had been to train a roomful of people of mixed abilities, and I thought companies might find it useful for pre-screening the delegates they sent on courses. This was my new business, and I called it Silver Linings Solutions because it seemed appropriate for me at the time.

Our technology was popular and we sold it into large organisations, including police forces and the NHS. Our big break came when the O2 mobile network gave us a £200,000 order. This enabled me to get back on my feet financially and to buy my own home again; in fact it's where I still live today, with offices in an extension.

It also gave me some headroom to think. I hadn't yet had a chance to learn all the lessons from the mistakes in my first business, but having had the experience of losing my house, I knew that I didn't want to risk my own money again. So I decided to look for venture capitalists and went on a programme at Warwick University which taught me how to persuade investors to buy into my business. I finished in the top three on the course, which meant that I was entered into the Midlands £1 Million Investment Challenge. This involved me pitching to 300 investors, with one of us receiving £1 million of investment capital. And that winner was me!

I didn't receive the million pounds in one go, although I did get £250,000 in the first tranche. This brought my share of the business down from 98 per cent to 40 per cent – a steep reduction. But at least I had money to spend and the upshot was that, although the business didn't scale as quickly as my first company, it did extremely well. Building on our success with O2, we went on to acquire lucrative contracts with Orange and other telecommunications companies; soon we found ourselves supplying global brands with our innovative software.

However, working with finance from venture capitalists was a frustrating experience because so much control was taken away from me. Mindful of how I'd neglected to grow my senior management team at Start-Right, I used some of their money to bring in a number of heavyweight people to the business. I intended to recruit two or three people, but the investors took over and employed a host of top-level executives. Within a few months, Silver Linings went from being just the two of us to having a crazy number of senior staff, with a vice-president of this and a president of that. This made the company too top heavy to fulfil its true potential. A regular day would be spent in meeting after meeting, picking apart decisions ad infinitum instead of getting things done. It couldn't have been more different to the culture I'd fostered at Start-Right.

In the end, my heart wasn't in it. My alarm clock would go off in the morning and I'd have to drag myself out of bed – that had never happened before. And because we had surplus cash we weren't hungry enough, so there was no urgency to grow profitable revenue. It didn't feel like my company anymore, and I decided to walk away. As it happened, some years after I left, Silver Linings was eventually sold for $8.9 million. That sounds like a lot, but given its original potential and investment level, it was disappointing. After tax and costs I only received around $100,000.

Before I made the break, I needed to solve the problem of not having enough money of my own (Silver Linings was cash rich, but I wasn't). So I did what I always do when I have my back to the wall: I spotted another opportunity. Marketing was the most important skill I'd developed in both my companies, and I loved it. Reckoning that there was a need for other small business owners to up their marketing game, I set up my own marketing consultancy on the side – my third start-up. Two people joined me: Danny, who was at Silver Linings, and my sister Hilary. Over the next two years the consultancy thrived, but I only ever saw it as a short-term move to earn enough cash for what I wanted to do next. This was to develop the technology for what became my fourth business, Smart Apprentices.

Smart beginnings

Three of my four children went to university but one was of a practical inclination and did an apprenticeship instead. However, he was more practical than academic and didn't enjoy writing up his assignments. This was made worse by the cumbersome nature of apprentice training, which involved a raft of paperwork. 'Surely there's a better way,' I thought. 'Why not get rid of all the paperwork and put it in the cloud?' I realised that I'd spotted a gap in the market, so I started to sketch out some ideas for a web-based platform to sell to colleges. My plan would give both apprentice trainers and their learners what they needed in an easy-to-access way. Smart Apprentices was born.

Everything seemed aligned for success. I had some money put aside from my consultancy earnings so I didn't have to take out a loan or put my house on the line. And after my experience with Silver Linings, I definitely didn't want to go down the equity financing route. Together with Danny and Hilary, I decided to enhance the initial software offshore so that we could get it to market quickly, using customer feedback to develop it from there.

I also realised something that hadn't occurred to me when I set up my first three businesses: that I needed to start with the exit in mind. With Start-Right I'd not given it a moment's thought and my market ended up crumbling around me. With Silver Linings I wasn't in control of when and how I would exit because of the venture capitalists. And my marketing consultancy would never have been a sellable proposition because it relied on me to deliver the service. But with Smart Apprentices, I promised myself it would be different. 'When and how will I exit from this business?' I thought. I was in my late 40s, with few assets and a massive mortgage, and was ploughing every penny I earned into the business. It was then that I decided my goal was to set up and manage Smart Apprentices in such a way that at the end of seven years I could sell up and never have to work again.

Time to grow

We did our market research first, of course – that much I'd learned from my previous experiences. We discovered that we weren't the first apprentice e-portfolio product on the market, but that all the others did was mirror the manual, paper-based process and store it online – there was no genuine innovation. What's more, the day-to-day work of an apprentice trainer seemed to be incredibly inefficient. They'd get in their car to visit a student's workplace, carrying a folder stuffed with sheets of paper that might get lost or damaged. Or, if they had access to an e-portfolio service, they'd log on to that while they were on site. Either way, the most they could manage would be a couple of visits a day.

We decided to go one step further and ask ourselves how we could transform the sector by making fuller use of technology. That's why we included the Smart Rooms element of our system, which was a web-based conferencing facility and one of our main points of difference.

Our goal was to disrupt the marketplace by cutting across the standard working practices of apprenticeship training.

We moved fast, starting in October 2010 and putting the technology out by April 2011. I believed then, and still do, that there's a 'now time' for any innovative product or service, and I didn't want that window of opportunity to close. Because this type of technology wasn't completely new, our customers' hearts and minds had already opened up to it, which meant that we didn't face a battle to get them interested. At the same time, we offered a fresher product than our competitors.

You'll not be surprised to learn it wasn't all plain sailing. We had our share of challenges in the early years – including a dirty tricks campaign from one of our mainstream competitors, an evacuation order from our offices by local planning officials and a major flaw in our software which temporarily rendered it unusable. This last crisis was the only time I felt like giving up, but I'm nothing if not resilient and tenacious. With the help of an IT consultant called Andy we fixed the problem without losing any customers or staff, and were delighted to welcome him into the fold as our first IT director.

Time for something different

Despite managing to leap over those hurdles without injuring myself too badly, I realised that they'd revealed gaps in my knowledge about how to grow a business quickly but in a sustainable way. It had been relatively easy to get Smart Apprentices to increase its turnover by over ten times in the first couple of years. Actually, pretty much anyone can do that. And once a business is at that level, it's not too difficult to grow it slowly year on year by 5 or 10 per cent. But, I asked myself, what's the smoothest way of getting to over £1 million profit? After all, making high profits rapidly is the holy grail of all businesses. And why do some businesses achieve this while others don't? When I realised that I didn't have all the answers, I decided to do an MBA.

It was challenging because there was a lot of reading, and (as you may have guessed) I'm easily bored. My main piece of work was my dissertation, for which I researched literature on business growth and interviewed high-growth business owners. (Its title is 'Characteristics Influencing High Growth in Technology Companies Selected for Inclusion in the 2014 Sunday Times Tech Fast Track 100'. I never said it was catchy.) I wanted to learn what factors influenced rapid growth so that I could emulate those characteristics in Smart Apprentices. Even though I'd had the tenacity to build all four of my businesses, I still hadn't broken through the ceiling of having a super-high growth company without putting the fundamentals at risk. I wanted to know the secret, and you can read my research findings towards the end of this book if you're interested to learn more.

In the end, it took me ten years to grow and sell

Smart Apprentices, but it was a good exit – ideal, in fact. I'm now spending my time how I like and am, you'll not be surprised to know, in the process of launching a number of new ventures. The difference with these is twofold: they're in service of me supporting other entrepreneurs rather than myself, and they're benefiting from the valuable lessons I've learned from my entrepreneurial career.

That's why I've written this book – to help you to achieve the same freedom. I would never tell you exactly what to do because there are a thousand ways of starting, scaling and selling a business. But there are some key elements that you must get right if you're to wake up one morning to see that money in your bank account like I did.

The book is split into three parts: Start, Scale and Sell. In each of these I walk you through the main areas to focus on if you're to progress to the next level. Because what got you here won't necessarily get you there, which means that you need to become a new kind of entrepreneur at each stage.

What you'll learn is largely based on my own experience. But so that it's not only me you're listening to, I've interviewed other business owners who've also successfully exited their companies. They were kind enough to give me their advice, born from years of risk-taking, triumphs and failures, and I can't thank them enough for sharing it with me. You'll see it interspersed throughout the book, and I hope that you find it useful.

I know that you're a fast mover so I won't keep you any longer. Let's dive in.

PART 1

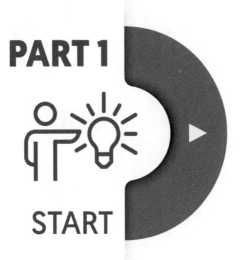

START

1

The One Decision

When you went through the process of setting up your business, I expect that there were many questions on your mind:

↗ What kind of company should it be?
↗ How do I bring my first customers on board?
↗ Where can I get money from?
↗ Why is everything more complicated than I thought?

But if you're like the majority of entrepreneurs, the one question you didn't ask yourself was: 'Do I want to sell this business at some point?'

It's understandable because at the beginning there are many other things to think about, and the idea that there may be an end to your business seems unreal. When I launched my first venture, I didn't even know it was possible to sell it – nothing could have been further from my mind. Even with my second one, I assumed that I would carry on running it until some unspecified time in the future, after which... who knew? It was only when I started my most recent business, Smart Apprentices, that I decided right from the beginning that my aim was to sell it within a set number of years.

Why sell, and why decide now?

Why sell your company at all? There's nothing that says you have to – in fact most owners don't, either because it doesn't occur to them or because they're happy with a lifestyle business that gives them the income and flexibility they desire. But if you're curious about the benefits of selling up, the following are the two main ones that I can think of.

It monetises your hard work

I don't need to tell you what a roller coaster launching and managing a start-up is. I can't imagine anybody doing it as an easy career option – you'd have to be crazy to think that way. Long hours, financial risk, endless stress, punctuated by – thankfully – the joys that come with successes along the road. So when you put that much into it, why limit your reward to the money you earn while running it? Why not also give yourself the opportunity to land an amazing deal at the end, which potentially nets you millions of pounds and sets you up for the rest of your life? Sure, it's a lot of work to sell, but by the time you get to that stage it will be just one more business challenge – and you'll be used to those.

It prepares you to explore new opportunities

When you first start your company it can be almost impossible to imagine your life without it. It's a massive part of who you are and what you do – you can never switch off from it. And yet it's not your alter ego; it's a company that's separate from yourself. That means you have to think about what you want to do when you're no longer in charge. What else do you want to achieve with your life, apart from steering your business to success?

When you know from early on in your entrepreneurial journey that there will come a day when you sell up, you're acknowledging that your involvement won't be without end. That prepares you for the time when you can do different things. For instance, I volunteered for the Samaritans charity during the later stages of running Smart Apprentices because I was interested to see what I could give back to the community in the future. I was laying the groundwork for when I wouldn't be running my business anymore, and I'm glad that I did because it meant I could embark on my new life much more easily after I exited.

Nowadays I'm enjoying exploring various experiences because I have the time to devote to them; they include inspiring and mentoring young entrepreneurs and investing in other people's businesses. Doing this without being burdened by the responsibility of running my company has made all the difference because while I was still in it I didn't have the head space for new things.

So those are the two main reasons for selling your business. However, it's not just a question of 'if' but also 'when'. There are benefits to making the choice at the beginning, rather than doing what most people do, which is to leave it to nearer the end. Of course, you can decide then if you want, but you'll find yourself wishing that you'd thought about it earlier. This is something I learned through the disappointing ways that my first two ventures came to a close. It's a different ball game to set up a company with the intention of selling it than it is to set one up without that conscious goal. In fact, to my mind, deciding whether or not to sell is as fundamental a part of starting a company as developing your product and finding the right customers for it. Here's why.

It means you set things up right

Buyers of businesses have certain requirements that need to be met if they're to make you a good offer, and you'll find it a lot harder to meet those requirements if you haven't set up your company in the right way to begin with. We'll explore what those requirements are as we go through the book, but for now just know that it's well worth creating a business that's 'sellable' as opposed to one that isn't. The last thing you need at the point when someone expresses an interest is to embark on a panic retrofitting spree to correct all the elements that make your company less attractive to the buyer. Especially as some things aren't possible to fix at that stage.

It means that you're more likely to have a successful sale

What would a 'good' sale look like to you? For me it was a combination of three things:

↗ achieving as high a valuation as possible
↗ not having to carry on working in the business after it was sold
↗ selling to a buyer who would look after my company.

What's most important to you? The second point is especially relevant when you're early on in your venture. I have many entrepreneur friends who, having sold their companies, were given no choice by their buyers but to stay on and carry out an earn-out for anything between two and five years. They weren't given the option of walking away with full cash, thereby monetising the whole of their equity in one go. You might like the idea of staying on, especially if you're deeply attached to your business, but most founders find that their enthusiasm wanes once their buyer is calling the shots. The more you can put in place at the beginning to avoid this, the better because there are very few earn-outs that work well for either the entrepreneur or the investor.

To summarise, you don't *have* to sell your business. In fact you could carry on running it forever, which many founders do. It can be hard to leave: you're no longer the boss, with a purpose and an agenda for your day. Instead, you wake up in the morning and there are all sorts of choices about what you could do. If you're the kind of person who finds that fun, it may be for you, but if not, you might be better off staying put. However, if you do want to sell then it makes a huge difference to how successful the sale will be if you decide it from the start. When I launched my first two ventures I didn't understand how the mechanics of selling worked, and I paid the price. Now I know different, and I'm hoping that what you'll learn in the rest of this book will guide you in the right direction.

Who will buy your business?

If you've decided that selling is for you, you might be thinking about who would buy your business. At launch stage you don't need to know exactly who you're going to sell to – that's way ahead in the future. But it does help to have a rough idea because it can make a difference to the decisions you make today. What kind of buyer will you look for when the time comes? There are three main options:

↗ a management buyout, in which your senior leadership team (or part of it) raises the finance to buy out your shares
↗ a purchase by a private equity firm or investment house
↗ a purchase by another company aligned with the same market as you; this is often called a 'trade exit'.

Management buyouts are rare because they depend on the company's senior team not only wanting to own the business themselves, but also being able to raise enough money. And while selling to a private equity firm or investment house is more common, they'll only be acquiring your business equity, which means that you'll be unlikely to receive the best value. Also, they're not interested in running your business, which means that you'll definitely be asked to stay on for some time. Most companies that sell on advantageous terms for the founder do so through a trade exit, which means being acquired by another firm that has a close alignment with the same market as you do. That's how I sold Smart Apprentices. Your buyer is likely to be significantly larger than you and to have deeper pockets. It may be a competitor which finds you a threat to its existence, especially if you've done a better job of solving a problem in your market than it has. It would rather buy you out than keep trying to stay ahead of you, and the most cost-effective way of doing that is to bring your product into its portfolio. That way, your competitor not only gains access to your product but also to your expertise, resources and customers. Well-known examples of this are Facebook's acquisition of Instagram and WhatsApp.

So I'd advise that you look at a trade exit as your most lucrative way out. You may already have thought of a couple of likely names but I suggest that you keep an open mind, because it's not only competitors who may be interested. You might find that you win attention from a business having a synergy with your own, such as when eBay acquired PayPal and when Microsoft bought Skype. The overarching point is that by thinking now about who may buy you, you're starting with the end in mind. This enables you to put the right elements in place for selling your company one day in the future.

Timescales

As soon as you start thinking about selling, you're bound to set a mental timescale. But, as with so many other things in business, the date of the sale is unlikely to be your choice – the stars must align in your favour. It takes a long time to get your company to the point at which it's sellable, usually between 8 and 12 years, although a few manage it more quickly. And there will be a window of opportunity for selling which won't be open forever. You might have launched your business with an innovative product or service at a time when your market wasn't crowded, but by ten years down the line, despite your efforts to refresh, pivot and develop it, more competitors have come into your space and you're finding it harder to differentiate yourself. This was my experience with Smart Apprentices; there were twice as many competitors in our market when I exited as when I started. You need to sell when your market is still attractive to a buyer.

Another reason for the window of opportunity closing is that you might not have kept up to speed with developments in your area and could be in danger of becoming irrelevant. This is, of course, an excellent reason for scaling and selling your business in the first place. There are few markets that don't shift over time, and today it's happening more quickly than ever. You can't afford to be bypassed by new technology and lose the opportunity to sell for a high value.

What problem are you solving?

I started this chapter by talking about one of the key decisions you need to make when you launch your start-up: whether or not you intend to sell it. The next one you should make is this: *what problem your product is solving*. I ask all the entrepreneurs I meet about this, and I find the answers revealing because they give me an insight into how well thought through their business ideas are. Your product not only needs to solve a problem, but the problem must have certain qualities if it's to be the foundation for your company's success. What could those qualities be?

The problem must be painful enough

Not all problems are created equal. Think about an issue that's troubling you right now – how big a deal is it to you? Is it urgent? Is it super painful? And most importantly, is it something you'd be willing to spend money on solving?

As an example, like many people I do my grocery shopping online. What I often find is that my regular online provider doesn't stock a couple of my favourite products, so I have to visit a physical store to buy them. This is a problem for me, and if an entrepreneur was to come up with a solution (for instance, a service which collects the missing items from the bricks-and-mortar store and adds them to my online shop delivery) I might be interested. But only if it's low cost; I don't find the situation annoying enough to be willing to pay more than a small amount for the benefit. Given that, I'd be unlikely to be a profitable customer for this new business.

You can work out how painful a problem is for your potential customers by looking at how they're solving it already. If they're not doing anything about it, that's either because they're not bothered by it or don't see it as a problem in the first place. When I started Smart Apprentices, the problem I was solving was that of colleges and apprentices storing assessment paperwork in physical folders which could get lost and weren't accessible to people in different locations at the same time. If I'd discovered that there was no appetite for solving this problem I'd have abandoned my idea at once, but I could see that there was a market for it because some colleges with apprenticeship programmes were investing time and money on other digital solutions. They were using Excel spreadsheets, Word documents and Google Docs, which of course were cumbersome and not nearly as user friendly as my idea.

The problem must matter to enough people

You can tell whether there's a big enough market for your product by researching how many competitors are already in that space. Ideally you want a small number, enough to show that there's an appetite for it but not so many that it's overcrowded. When I launched Smart Apprentices there were a few competitors in existence, but they were quite basic providers that only took the paper documents and stored them online. So I could see that the market was ripe for a more innovative player that would transform how learners were assessed and managed.

The problem must be one you can solve

Your capabilities and experience are critical here. Do you have some kind of personal experience related to your product which means that you're the right person to develop it? In my case I'd been a college lecturer in the past, had a son who'd been through an apprenticeship scheme and was also the parent of four children who'd travelled through the education system. That meant I had a clear insight into the issues caused by relying on paperwork or an unwieldy patchwork of other solutions. If I hadn't had this experience, I'd have had to work a lot harder to understand the problem my product was solving. Ask yourself if you're the best person to launch your business, or whether your energies would be best spent elsewhere.

You can see how your problem must be:

↗ painful enough
↗ widespread enough
↗ solvable by you.

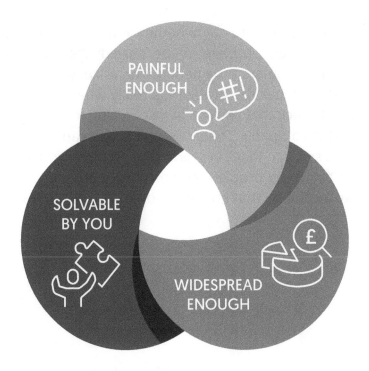

If your product doesn't solve a problem that's painful

enough, that's experienced by enough people and that doesn't make use of your specific experiences and talents, your business will be unlikely to succeed. All the time, I come across entrepreneurs who don't think this through. Many don't see themselves as solving a problem but as developing something new. Usually they haven't researched whether the problem is already being solved in a different way or whether it's painful enough for people to want to invest in it. Nor do they know how many people are suffering because of it. This is particularly common with technology entrepreneurs, who can find it difficult to see beyond their product and its features to what the problem is that they're trying to solve.

It's not for you to say whether you think there's a painful enough problem to be solved; it's for your potential customers – the people who will pay for it. Ask yourself whether the problem is really what you think it is, and check that you're not just looking for a reason to start a company. The worst thing you can do is to create a solution that's in search of a problem; you need to start with the problem and *then* work out if you can create a solution that enough people will want to buy.

Quick recap

- ↗ You don't have to sell your business, but there are advantages if you do.
- ↗ If you do want to sell, it's worth deciding this at the beginning rather than leaving it until later.
- ↗ Keep an open mind about who might buy your company and when.
- ↗ Make sure that your product is solving a problem that's painful and widespread enough for people to want to pay to solve it.

Questions to ask yourself

- ↗ Do I want to sell my business? Is that my aim?
- ↗ What sort of timescale am I looking at?
- ↗ Who might buy it?
- ↗ What problem am I solving?
- ↗ Is it painful and widespread enough?
- ↗ Am I the right person to solve it?

An Entrepreneur's Experience

Tom Carroll

Tom has worked in the IT sector for over 30 years, starting and selling three very different IT businesses. One was a software company that developed solutions for the clothing and textile industry. One was an e-commerce business that supplied luxury pet products. And one was an IT service business that supplied outsourced IT services and complex project delivery. All of them had one thing in common: a great team of people who cared about the quality of what they were delivering to their clients. Today he's not stopped working because, in his words, 'it's in my nature to always be chasing something. I find it interesting, and I like the win.'

Tom shared with me the lessons he's learned about starting, scaling and selling a business. Here are some of the highlights.

Don't try to be too clever

One of my early mistakes in business was trying to be far, far too clever. At the time of my first IT company, Windows was at 3.1 – the first incarnation of a Windows desktop. So what did we decide to do? Embed pictures and live video into the product sheets. What's more, we didn't realise that the PCs that would run our software only had two megabytes of memory, which meant that we launched a product which had to run on infrastructure that wasn't fit for purpose. This caused us three years of pain, which was difficult but taught me a really good lesson: never, ever be too confident about what you're doing. If you don't have the money, don't go leading edge; it's reckless and you can destroy everything.

Provide a clear point of difference for your service

My second business was an IT support company which I bought in its infancy, calling it Our IT Department. We were different to our competitors in that we didn't offer a range of services designed to suit individual customer groups, but one really high-quality service that worked for everyone. This was to fix IT problems as quickly as possible while keeping our clients informed about where we were at. Unusually for the time, we also focused on preventative maintenance. We were early adopters of monitoring tools that could predict problems in advance, which meant that our clients had fewer emergencies. This benefited both them and us, as we could reduce our random use of high-end engineering, and it made us more profitable.

Use client attrition as an opportunity to learn

The client base for Our IT Department grew rapidly and soon we were taking on a new business every week. But we had to retain them – there was no point in recruiting a client and losing an existing one at the same time. If we lost a client, we'd have a thorough post-mortem. We didn't point fingers and hang people off a scaffold, but we did have a lack of tolerance for the situation. This meant fixing the reasons why they'd left us at a systemic level, rather than looking at individual people. The result of this was that we didn't lose any clients at all for many years unless they'd been acquired or gone out of business.

When you have a great product and

great marketing, sales will come

I didn't start out as a 'complete' business person – marketing in particular was something I had to learn about. At first I assumed that I'd just hire great salespeople and that would be the answer, but I discovered that they can be high maintenance and don't always deliver. I stumbled around in the dark for years trying to get sales teams to work with telesales teams and direct sales teams, and so on. That took me a while to understand, and slowly but surely I realised that the trick to making sales was marketing. If you have a good product and you get the message out there, almost anyone can sell the product if they understand it. Once I had that up and running, I changed the kind of salespeople I employed so that they were more consultative and could sell in a sincere way; this also reflected my own ethos. I came to see marketing as an investment rather than a cost.

The best time to sell your business is when you have the right offer

Eventually a bigger fish bought me. The owners approached me, even though I wasn't thinking of selling at the time; I could see that they wanted to make a serious offer and were genuine about it. From this I learned that you shouldn't specify when you want to sell your business, such as when it reaches a certain turnover, because you don't know where the market will be at that stage and who will be interested. The time to sell is when you have the right offer.

2

Start-up Fundamentals

I think of the start-up phase as being the first three or four years. During that time your business will grow from being the founder (or founders) with no turnover and zero value to a completely different entity altogether. At launch, Smart Apprentices was made up of only three of us, but by the time we hit our fourth birthday we numbered a dozen people and were turning over £1.5 million. Not only had we ramped up our customer base, but we'd also 'grown up' culturally. We had systems and processes in place and were looking to formalise our senior team.

But let's not get too far ahead of ourselves. What I'm focusing on in this chapter are the fundamentals you need to put in place in the early years. You have your product idea and you're confident that it solves a painful problem, but what else should you be thinking about? We're going to explore:

↗ finding your niche
↗ becoming a marketing expert
↗ selling your minimum viable product (MVP)

↗ raising money
↗ recruiting your initial team
↗ putting in place contracts and legalities
↗ looking after your own wellbeing.

Finding your niche

If you want to sell for as high a value as possible, it's essential to enter your market within the right niche or segment. Many start-ups think they can offer their product or service to 'everyone' or that they can capture a small percentage of the entire sector. As an investor now, I see many pitches in which the founders claim that their market is worth £X million and that they can easily snare X per cent of it.

This is a crazy mistake to make. No market is homogenous; if you look closely, you'll see that there are many different customer types within it. None of us uses the same thing in the same way. For instance, many of us have an Alexa device from Amazon, but have different reasons for buying it. Also, some of us are early adopters who are happy to splurge on new technology despite the risks, whereas others take longer to warm up to innovations and are more price conscious. If you want 1 per cent of your market, which 1 per cent is it?

You need to identify the niche that's right for you. Given your product and the problem it solves, who will see it as most valuable? Who will pay a premium for it because it delivers what they want? Pick a segment within your sector and research it to death. Test and measure it. And once you've made your choice, stick with it unless you have a very good reason not to.

So niching is essential, but what makes a good niche? It has four key characteristics:

↗ It makes use of your personal values, skills and expertise as a founder.
↗ It's large enough for a new entrant.
↗ It's accessible.
↗ It receives your laser-like focus at all times.

It makes use of your personal values, skills, and expertise

Although you're not the only person in your business, as the founder your character percolates through it and therefore has an impact on who you're best placed to sell to. At Smart Apprentices we first focused on a premium niche of the largest 150 of the 3,500 apprentice training providers in the UK. Part of the reason for this was that earlier in my career I'd had plenty of experience working in (and selling to) sizeable organisations with a hierarchical management structure. It didn't faze me to walk into a boardroom and present my product to a row of suits because I knew from experience that I could work well with them.

It's large enough

Is your niche large enough to fit with your business aspirations? If your plan is to create and sell a £10 million revenue business, but your segment is only worth £40 million, you'll need to own 25 per cent of it. That's a huge proportion and probably not realistic. It's easy to be overoptimistic about how much market share you can gain, so be sure that your market size aligns with your ambitions.

It's accessible

How will you find a route into your segment? How accessible is it? And how crowded does it look to be – is there any 'white space' left for you to fill? There's no point in trying to enter a niche that's already fully occupied unless you're sure you have something far better to offer.

Part of what makes a niche accessible is when customers within it network with each other. Once Smart Apprentices started to become accepted by the top 150 colleges, those colleges talked to each other. Some even held events to show other large institutions how they were benefiting from our platform because they believed in it so much. They knew that if we were successful we'd continue to grow our technology, an outcome that they wanted as much as we did.

It receives your laser-like focus at all times

One afternoon, around three years after Smart Apprentices had been launched, my business development manager came to me full of excitement. He'd discovered an opportunity to sell to a new group of institutions that we hadn't approached before. I had no hesitation in deciding whether or not to go for this: the answer was 'no'. It would be, as I explained to him, a distraction.

When he asked why, I answered that even though our business was still small and we had little cash in the bank, dominating the segment we'd chosen was our overriding priority. If we said 'yes' to customers who weren't in our segment, we'd be diverting our finite time and resources away from the ones who were. We wouldn't be able to devote ourselves to understanding our core customers' problems and improving our product for them. This laser focus gave us a critical advantage. We made ourselves extremely difficult to compete with in our niche because we became the go-to experts in it, with the strongest brand. And we achieved this because instead of trying to spread ourselves around all 3,500 members of our potential customer base, we were famous with the top 150.

This is so difficult, and yet so essential, to do. Chasing customer numbers is vanity – it's about wanting to be well known across your sector. But your aim shouldn't be to be popular across the board – only with the people in your niche. If people outside it have never heard of you, so what? It's more important to be the best-kept secret of the customers you want to have than for everyone else to be talking about you. And that involves saying no to many opportunities.

Becoming a marketing expert

Focusing on a tight niche makes just as much sense when it comes to your marketing because if you're only talking to a small number of customers you're in a great position to create a rock-solid brand. Your marketing will be smarter and more cost effective, and more likely to be remembered, than if you spread yourself too thinly.

Marketing is also the area in which you can burn the most money as a start-up. There's a company that I was considering investing in recently but I've decided not to. Its cost of customer acquisition is £43 but the average lifetime value of a customer is only £32. How does that make sense? The reality is that you don't need to spend as much money on marketing as you think. When I started my first business, the computer training company, I won my first huge contract by training just one senior person and within three years I'd covered his whole workforce. I landed that initial deal simply by chatting to their HR director about what pain points the business had as part of my market research. I wasn't even trying to sell, and I certainly didn't spend any cash.

I've never met an entrepreneur who has this mindset. People seem to think that they need to plough large sums into SEO, paid-for advertising and content generation. It's as if they look at the marketing tools available and work out how much they can afford to spend, often focusing exclusively online and forgetting other channels. But here's the thing: that's what everyone else is doing. You have to be fresh and different, so think about how you can stand out by marketing in a new way. One of the best options is to find what I call your customers' watering holes.

Find your customers' watering holes

How can you talk to the key people in your segment so that they know you're solving their problem better than anyone else? The answer is to find the places where they hang out, both online and offline, such as forums, social media groups, networking events and conferences. These are their watering holes.

Bear in mind that your segment will include different groups of people, each with their own gathering place.

For instance, in our focused market of large apprentice-ship providers, one type of potential customer was the head of management information systems (MIS). We knew that these people were mostly male, in their late thirties onwards and pretty senior at work. They weren't likely to be on Facebook or Twitter, and were also quite introverted. That meant that we were most likely to find them buried away in the depths of a professional body such as the British Computer Society or as members of college associations which had a special interest group for technology experts. To reach them, we became associate members of some professional bodies so that we could interact within their world.

Get your messaging right

Your next step is to create marketing messages that resonate individually with the different groups in your segment. If you communicate in the same way across the board just because it's easy, your messages will fall on fallow ground. Your company has a solution to a problem, but to the various types of people you're aiming at, that problem may look completely different. The main concern for a head of MIS, for instance, was to avoid any technical issues when installing a new system, especially if they'd had problems with a previous one. Our messages to that group therefore focused on how robust our platform was and the rigorous processes we had to ensure that their data wouldn't be compromised.

You don't always have to think 'sales' when you spread your marketing messages either. You can deliver information and content that's nothing to do with your product but is still relevant in some way. For instance, in the early years of Smart Apprentices I'd visit our customer colleges and give a talk about entrepreneurship to their students called 'Who Wants to be a Millionaire?'. It would take me a couple of hours plus preparation and travel, but it was fun and the students found it aspirational. What did it say to our customers about our brand? That we were successful and growing quickly in the technology space. It also helped us to make a name for ourselves with the senior leadership team at large colleges because I became 'the CEO who came in and did that talk'. You can do anything, as long as it fits with your brand and is in tune with your skill set – it's just another way of spending time at your customers' watering holes.

Underpinning your messaging is your brand. Is it instantly recognisable and relevant for its market? We presented the Smart Apprentices brand as premium to suit the segment we'd chosen. For instance, when we sent out a physical mailing (because our competitors all sent emails and we wanted to stand out), we made sure that our envelopes were tasteful and that the addresses were typed onto them, not stuck on with a label. We even sent out mailings when the new stamp collections came out so that they would look well presented. And we thought of every touchpoint, so our trainers wore branded polo shirts whenever they visited a potential customer. Our attention to detail was constantly reinforcing our brand.

This sounds like common sense, but I know that most start-ups focus more on their product and processes than they do on their target customers. To them, marketing is collateral: websites, social media posts and the like. However, your marketing materials should be the last of them, and in any case, you can't develop them if you don't know your core messages in the first place. What does your marketing need to look like and say so that it speaks directly to the people you want to influence?

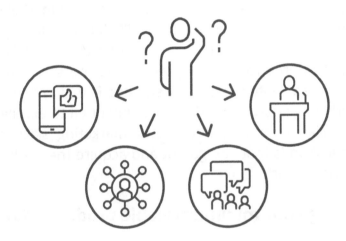

Sales will follow

The good news is that, if you get your marketing right, sales are relatively easy to come by. Founders often put sales before marketing, lump them together or focus purely on sales. But if you've done your marketing properly, when you contact a prospect directly it's easy to engage them because they already recognise your brand and understand what problem you solve. They're likely to want to talk to you, and it's a straightforward conversation to have. So marketing comes before sales, not at the same time, and certainly not the other way around.

Because of the importance of marketing, it follows

that every founder should know how to market their business. You can have the best product targeted at the right segment, but if no one knows about it you'll end up running out of money. Many entrepreneurs have a love–hate relationship with marketing, so if you're not confident with it you must learn how to be. Of course you can bring in external support, but good marketing people are expensive. And how will you know if they're doing a great job? The main thing I did differently at Smart Apprentices to my previous businesses, and to which I attribute most of my success, is that I used the marketing knowledge I'd built up and put it to excellent use. Like it or not, if you lack marketing skills my suggestion is that you go out and acquire them – both online and off.

Selling your minimum viable product (MVP)

At Smart Apprentices, I didn't take any external investment, mainly because I didn't want to be beholden to investors in the same way as I'd been at Silver Linings. But what I didn't appreciate was how much of an edge this would give us in terms of our product development. We didn't have the luxury of sitting down and creating the perfect product before we went to market, so within six months we'd developed an MVP (minimum viable product) and sold it to some early adopters. This gave us three key advantages:

↗ It created a sense of urgency.
↗ We made a better product because it was based on customer feedback rather than our own idea of what was right.

↗ It focused our minds on earning money rather than spending it.

Let's explore these excellent reasons for getting your product out there as quickly as you can.

A sense of urgency

A key danger in an early start-up is being scared of launching. I understand why – it feels vulnerable to put your product out there, so you spend time perfecting it instead. I'll admit it takes a degree of confidence to put an incomplete product into the market, but having no cash to play with is a great way of overcoming your fears. After all, the start-up phase is all about securing revenue from early adopters, looking after them and then targeting similar-profile customers. So why wait?

A better product

Who's the best person to decide if your new product is good enough? You? Your IT chief? Your marketing officer? The answer is that it's none of these people. The best person to tell you whether your product is brilliant or could do with improvement is your customer. Customers and users – in other words, the people who pay for your product – know far better than you whether it will solve their problems well enough. So it makes sense that putting your product into the marketplace and gaining early feedback is a much better use of your time than spending months and months perfecting it. Because what does perfection even look like? You can't know, but your customers will.

Let's say you're starting a smoothie company on a

subscription model. You might only have one or two flavours to begin with, so you target the early adopters who are likely to buy those flavours and who will give you feedback. That brings in some revenue, so you can now start to develop more varieties. You're keeping focused on your customers.

I should add a caveat here, which is that although your MVP can be basic, it does have to work and be robust. People are paying for it so it needs to do its job; it just doesn't need all the bells and whistles at this stage.

Financial independence

In my Silver Linings business, which was private equity financed, we took investment early on. It seemed that we were forever going through a funding round, spending the money on product development and then going through another round. We were getting money and then developing the product, rather than gaining *customers who paid for the product* and going on to develop it.

Not only that, but it took us a long time to start making money because we wasted months developing features rather than solving our customers' problems (problems that they were prepared to pay to have solved). We overengineered our technology by adding more and more features, which made it complex to use and also more expensive to buy. It became a way of being, and I see so many start-ups do this.

At Smart Apprentices we didn't even consider that option – we just got on with the business of building relationships with customers and users. We gained some early adopters, who not only helped us to shape our product but also gave us traction in the marketplace. This helped us to self-finance the business from the start; we even returned a profit in our first year. That's not bad going.

Raising money

One of the first things that you're likely to think about when you launch is how you'll fund your business. It can seem as if it's of critical importance to have money, but it really isn't everything. If it was, no small business would be able to disrupt the market by competing with large businesses.

It's important not to see lack of funds as a barrier to growth. I realise that sounds easy to say, but if you allow yourself to think 'If only I had £5,000 I could double my sales', you'll never get anywhere. You may not have £5,000, but if you have £500 what could you do with that? It's this way of thinking that separates the frugal, fast-growth entrepreneur from the one who doesn't recognise that their own mental resources are their greatest asset.

It seems to be the trend for start-ups to go through multiple investment rounds right from their early days, generating eye-watering valuations that are completely unrealistic. I've sat in on many pitches for these and have seen slides showing wild predictions and lists of senior staff that would be more suited to an established corporate. This is not only unnecessary but harmful. It may be hard to believe, but there's such a thing as having too much money; it can be a distraction because it puts your focus on the wrong things. Instead of feeling hungry, which gives you a sense of urgency, you're liable to be too comfortable. And what do we do when we're comfortable? We spend time and energy on what we want rather than what we need. I've seen many a new business burn through crazy amounts of cash by hiring too many senior people or splashing out on marketing that doesn't work. Often this has been at the bidding of their investors rather than being what the founders wanted.

Which brings me on to the other problem with taking a tranche of investment early on: you end up with a smaller slice of the business when you exit. As I discovered when Silver Linings was sold, there's a significant difference between receiving 90 per cent of the proceeds of sale, which is the percentage I started with, and less than 5 per cent, which is what I ended up with after various investment rounds.

Raising it

Of course, you do need *some* money to start with. When I launched Smart Apprentices I remortgaged my home, which funded the software development at first. To pay my two members of staff I used the earnings from my marketing consultancy business, which I carried on working in during the first year. My advice would be to do something along these lines if you can because one of the things I've discovered with external funding is that you can never get it when you need it – I can guarantee that. It's far better to be self-sufficient if at all possible.

Having said that, at some point you might need an extra injection of cash, so let's look at the various sources of funding along with their pros and cons.

Supply it yourself. This may surprise or even scare you, but do you have any assets that you can sell? Is there any work that you can do on the side, like I did with my marketing consultancy? If you're still employed, can you take out a personal loan or remortgage your house? And what about cutting costs, such as switching to an interest-only mortgage?

The most significant advantages of using your own assets as funding are speed, equity retention and control because you don't have to wait for other people to make up their minds about whether your business is worth investing in. That makes it quicker for you to get your MVP out there, after which you'll find it easier to attract external investment. You'll be in good company, too. In my MBA research I asked a number of entrepreneurs running fast-growing businesses how they financed them, and most used their own savings or sold some assets before attracting equity investment.

One thing I'd advise against is borrowing money from friends and family. Partly because you may lose it and them as well (they're hard to replace). And partly because it alters the dynamic of your relationship in ways that you might not predict.

Take a bank loan. A loan can be hard to come by and you'll almost certainly need collateral to guarantee it, which can be risky and stressful. I discovered this after my first business collapsed and I had to sell my home to pay off a loan I'd taken out for training facilities. However, loans do leave you in control as you don't have external investors telling you what to do, and the interest is tax deductible. A loan is also better than an overdraft, which can be called in by your bank without notice. If you do choose to take out a business loan be careful not to give a personal guarantee unless you absolutely have to.

Crowdfunding. This is a recent type of funding source and is increasingly popular, with growing numbers of platforms to choose from. There are two types of crowdfunding, reward and equity. Reward is where people give you money in return for a future reward, such as product that is yet to be developed. Equity is the more common type of crowdfunding for start-ups, and is where people invest a small amount of money for a small share of your business. While crowdfunding can be an attractive form of raising money it can lead to a complex capital expenditure (capex) table (lots of small investors, often 20–30) and you will sell a relatively large portion of your company for a small amount of investment. While this wouldn't be my go-to option for raising early funding it shouldn't be discounted if you are struggling to get investment elsewhere.

Angel investors. These are high net worth individuals who invest in start-ups because of the huge tax benefits on offer. Their major downside is that they take some of your equity, which, given your business isn't worth anything at the beginning, will entail you giving away a large chunk of it for not much in return. However, angel investment can work if it's smart money, by which I mean that the investor adds something to your business in terms of expertise or opens doors for you. Generally, though, angel investors are hands off in their approach.

Venture capital funding. This is more relevant once you have a track record and have started to grow. Venture capital funders are similar to angel investors, but the main difference is that they have deeper pockets as they're investing their institution's money rather than their own. They tend to have a more businesslike approach to their relationship with you, demanding a larger slice of your company, harsher terms and probably a seat on your board. On the plus side, they're likely to have considerable expertise that's useful for a start-up business, especially if you pick a funder that's relevant to your sector. And as long as you hit your key performance indicators (KPIs) they're likely to stay with you, reinvesting in your subsequent funding rounds.

My experience of venture capital funding at Silver Linings was pretty negative; I lost the vast majority of my equity, and keeping our backers happy was a huge distraction. However, it might be a good option for you if you can make connections with other entrepreneurs whom your funders have also invested in, and also gain access to the expertise offered by a professional investor.

Grants. There are a number of government grants and bursaries that you can apply for. They're quite hard to obtain and don't represent a lot of money, but they do exist and are worth considering. However, I'd be cautious about chasing grants as they can be time consuming to apply for and a distraction from pursuing what you should be more interested in: revenue.

Recruiting your initial team

At the beginning of this chapter I mentioned that the business you start will be unrecognisable from the one it is when it's three or four years old. Nowhere is this more apparent than in the nature, and size, of your team. But what should that team consist of? Recruiting the right people to fill the right roles is a juggling act at first, but it helps to know that there are only a small number of 'seats' that you need fill in the early years:

↗ marketing
↗ sales
↗ finance
↗ operations
↗ product/tech.

MARKETING   SALES   FINANCE   OPERATIONS   PRODUCT
/TECH

The people who fill these seats don't all have to be employees; your finance seat, for instance, could be taken by your accountant. Nor do you need to recruit a set of full-time staff – indeed, you almost certainly can't afford to. Consider asking some people to join on a temporary basis, maybe on a three-month contract – that way you get to 'try before you buy'. At Smart Apprentices our first technology director, Andy, was somebody we initially brought in on a temporary basis for advice and guidance, and four years later he came to work for us full time.

However you recruit people, it's worth ensuring that they're who you need. Every single person who's involved in your business at the beginning has to be right because it's exhausting enough launching a company without being let down by people and correcting their mistakes. It's worth spending as much time as you need to vet and appraise anyone you bring into the business because it will save you a lot of heartache later.

Be professional

Maybe it's something to do with the scariness of launching a new venture, but when you're a start-up it's tempting to think that you want to run it like a family business. However, you're not a family. Your real family is the one you've known for years and who will stick with you through thick and thin – it's an entirely different relationship to the people in your start-up team. I'm not suggesting that you shouldn't be friendly with them, but you should never recruit someone because they're a mate. Think about what would happen if the relationship were to go sour. My best friend of 30 years came to work in my business and it caused mayhem when things went wrong between us and I had to buy him out. Fortunately we salvaged the relationship, but it will never be the same again.

Another reason not to see staff as friends or family is that a start-up is a rapidly changing entity; the people who join you at first almost certainly won't be the right people to take you to exit, or even to scale up with. When you begin, there are two best options for recruiting people. Either bring in those who you can develop into senior roles later or those who are right for now but accept that you may have to lose them (or find another role for them) when you scale. You need to be mentally prepared for this, and to be clear with them about it as well. Don't bring someone in as a director when you don't envisage them doing anything more than a management level job; be realistic with them and with yourself.

And finally, it's important not to recruit people like you. We all have a tendency to gravitate towards those who are similar to us, but if you do that you won't have enough diversity to innovate and be successful. You'll fall prey to 'groupthink' instead. For instance, in my current Start, Scale, Sell venture, we were recently discussing how we could help school leavers to learn about entrepreneurship. My assumption was that any young person would be grateful for a £3,000 bursary because I'd had no money when I was that age – it would have been transformational for me. But somebody else in my team, whose own child had learned a lot from an unpaid internship, suggested that would be more valuable instead. We look through the lenses of our own lives, so being exposed to different viewpoints is healthy. The last thing you want is for your people to validate your rubbish ideas – you need them to tell you that there are other ways of seeing things.

Putting in place contracts and legalities

In the early years it's unlikely that you'll be thinking much about contracts and legalities. That can come later, surely? Some of it can, but there are certain elements that are vital to have in place from the start. There's a significant difference in sale value for a business which can prove that it owns its intellectual property (IP) and has proper employee, supplier and customer contracts and one that doesn't. Don't be slapdash now and regret it later.

Employment contracts

Try to think of an employment contract being a bit like a prenuptial agreement – it's there to protect you (and the employee) if anything goes wrong. But your contracts are also important when it comes to selling your business. Are they compliant with employment legislation? Do they protect your IP? Your buyer will scrutinise them during the exit process and you can't afford to have any loose ends here.

Vested equity

Because of the rapidly changing nature of a start-up, it's important that if you give equity to anyone in part exchange for salary, it's vested. This means that the person doesn't receive their shares straightaway, but only when they hit their KPIs. It's a way of making sure that if someone isn't up to the job, they can't still keep a slice of your company. Also, make sure that your shareholder agreement with them is documented properly, so that you know what will happen to their shares if they don't perform or if they leave your business.

Intellectual property

Anybody you contract with, whether they be an advisor, a freelancer or an employee, will probably generate IP for you. This could include written materials, graphic designs and coding, among others. If you don't include a clause in their contracts stating that any IP they generate belongs to your business rather than to them, you could face serious problems down the line when your buyer does their due diligence and discovers that you don't own some of your business assets. It's the same with trademarks – make sure that you register them.

Customer contracts

Let's be realistic – you're probably not going to ask your very first customer to sign an intricate contract. But you need to make sure that all your customers after that have a robust agreement with you because if you don't, you'll be leaving yourself wide open to risk.

Given that you don't have the bandwidth to think about all this stuff in the early years, I suggest you create a checklist that you consult every time you bring in a new person or sign up a new customer. If it's not you who does this, it should be your operations person or whomever you trust to be systematic and organised enough for the job. I can't stress how much easier it is to get these things right from the beginning than to have a panic when you come to sell and realise that you don't have the right paperwork in place. It will also have a significant impact on how much you can sell your business for.

Looking after your wellbeing

Without you, your start-up is nothing. You're the visionary, the cheerleader, the fixer, the coordinator... the list goes on. If it sounds exhausting, that's because it is. I don't think anything can prepare you for the first few years of a rapidly growing start-up – it's probably more stressful than scaling up, and certainly than exit. You're working hand to mouth, never sure how the next set of bills is going to be paid, and you don't yet have a large enough team to delegate to. Instead, you're doing everything yourself (or it certainly feels like it). You're all over your customers, making sure that they're happy, and you're all over your product, making sure that it keeps working beautifully.

Because you're such an important part of your business, you have to keep yourself energised. That isn't easy when you're working long hours, seven days a week, and your world looks as if it's teetering on the brink of collapse on a regular basis. I can't say that I handled this stage very well myself, but there are a few things I learned which I'll share with you here.

Talk to people

This was pretty much the only thing I did to look after myself, and it was invaluable. I'm fortunate in that I'm close to my siblings and my adult children, so I was able to offload onto them and tell them when things were getting too much. Make sure that you have people you can talk to, too.

I remember when, about three years after I launched Smart Apprentices, we were starting to feel confident that the business was going to work. However, it was still reactive and pretty chaotic; no sooner had we bedded in one client than another came on board, and in the pressure of keeping up with the pace, our software development took a back seat. Finally it all caught up with us when a major technical flaw caused our system to slow down and keep resetting itself. For the next six weeks there were angry customers shouting at us and threatening to cancel their contracts. To make matters worse, we didn't have a clue how to fix it or how long it would take.

I spent this time in an absolute nightmare. My team were fully occupied with taking customer calls, while I briefed them daily to explain what we were doing to solve the problem. We brought in IT consultant after IT consultant, but still couldn't get to the bottom of why the system wasn't working. It was the closest I've ever come to giving up. I didn't eat or sleep properly, and for a company like ours, which cared so much about its customers, it was devastating. However, my kids were the ones who got me through it. My eldest (by that point living in Australia) sent me a postcard of Abraham Lincoln, a man who famously failed many times before he was elected president. I still have it now in a frame, and it brings tears to my eyes whenever I remember it arriving.

Take exercise

By the time I reached the scale-up phase I'd hired a personal trainer and was much more focused on my physical fitness. But in the early days it was a different story. People told me to take time out and get some fresh air, but how was I supposed to do that when there was so much going on? I was already working until three o'clock in the morning on many days.

However, don't go by my example. Work can be addictive because it gives you an adrenaline rush: 'I've got to finish this – just one more bit.' But when you do force yourself to close your laptop and take a short break, you feel so refreshed when you come back. It helps you to look at what you were doing in a different light, and problems become easier to solve.

Retain control

Your start-up can seem as if it owns you, but it doesn't. You own it. So it's worth trying to push back and control it as much as you can; you don't have to answer every email as it comes in, for instance. I know how hard this is to do, and sometimes it's impossible. But what you can do is to segment your time so you have a deadline for every task you carry out. Imagine that you're charging a customer for it. This will help you to value your time and energy so you can schedule in the occasional recovery hour into your day.

Quick recap

- ↗ For fast growth and high profits, aim your product at a tight niche.
- ↗ Targeted marketing is critical for your sales success.
- ↗ Don't wait for perfection – get your MVP out there as quickly as you can.
- ↗ Try to be as financially self-sufficient as possible.
- ↗ Recognise that your start-up team won't be the one that takes you through scale-up to exit.
- ↗ Don't forget to put in place contracts and agreements.

Questions to ask yourself

- ↗ What's the most appropriate and lucrative niche for me to sell to?
- ↗ How much do I know about marketing? Could I learn more?
- ↗ Could I sell my product now, or is perfectionism holding back?
- ↗ Who in my team has the potential to take the business further, and who doesn't?
- ↗ Can I look after myself better?

An Entrepreneur's Experience

Chris Morling

'I blame my dad,' says Chris. 'Ever since he bought me a ZX81 in 1981, I've been hooked on tech. It started with writing computing games as a hobby in my teens (I did eventually get a girlfriend) and carried on throughout my life.'

In 2008, and without any outside investment, Chris launched the financial product comparison site money. co.uk and sold it to Zoopla Property Group ten years later. Today he focuses on Studee, a platform that helps students to maximise the likelihood of them getting offers from their chosen universities abroad. He hopes to take some of what he's learned in the world of fintech and apply it to edtech.

Chris is a passionate advocate of 'we can if...' rather than 'we can't because...' And (in his own words) he loves to talk business, tech and philosophy with anyone daft enough to hang around long enough for the conversation. I asked him to share with me the lessons he's learned about starting, scaling and selling a business. Here are some of the highlights.

Have a goal, and a strategy for how to reach it, right from the start – don't just chase the new, fun thing

For the first five years I didn't have a coherent strategy – I had little direction. Even though we were profitable early on, it took me two years to recruit someone and then two years after that to recruit the next person. It wasn't until just before we launched money.co.uk that I had a mindset shift and realised I could achieve more if I had a bigger goal. I was up against companies like Moneysupermarket and Confused.com, but prior to that point I didn't even set my sights on being a competitor to them. I was just focusing on the next 'shiny thing'. That's a classic mistake entre-preneurs make at the start – to just go after the new, fun opportunity and not think about a longer-term goal.

Timing is critical when you launch a product

money.co.uk worked for many reasons, the first being that the timing was right. It was launched in the early days of affiliate marketing; we had a couple of competitors, but the whole model was fairly new. What's more, if you knew what you were doing or were willing to learn, you could quickly rank well on Google and get great value out of Google Ads (and similar ads on other search engines). Which is what we did. Not many people knew about those opportunities when they launched, so the traffic was super cheap.

Treat employees the way you would want to be treated and they'll reward you with high performance

It's a bit of a cliché but I think culture is driven from the top. I used to say that my parents didn't help me in any way because they're not entrepreneurial risk-takers – they very much follow the status quo. But actually they gave me everything because they instilled in me my value system, which is simply to treat people the way you want to be treated. That simple rule, which I've had from the start without realising it, is what employees want. The result was that in 15 years we had only about ten people leave the business. Some of that retention was because of my leadership, but if my management team hadn't also had the same values I don't think that the culture would have disseminated throughout the rest of the company.

Keep a role for yourself that you enjoy and can add value through

There's no set role for an entrepreneur, so do what you want to do and what enables you to add most value. If you love marketing, focus on marketing and bring in a CEO or MD to run the business. Also, don't feel embarrassed or guilty about not enjoying some things. For instance, I care passionately about my team but I don't enjoy HR-related processes like interviewing. Far better to recruit somebody else who can manage that and make it happen, then to give support where needed.

If you can't answer a question about your online business within two minutes, your reporting and analytics are not up to scratch

It took only three years for money.co.uk to go from £4–£5 million net profit to £12 million plus. That was down to the scalability of the business model, which meant that we didn't need a bigger team to reach and service more customers. What we did need was more people coming onto the website, so we had to get really good at marketing, tracking and analysis. That's the bit that a lot of entrepreneurs miss. Right from the start, even in my bad coding days, I was obsessed with tracking and analysis so that I could understand what marketing and website UX (user experience) was working and what wasn't.

This meant that we could answer any data-driven business question immediately. We knew, in real time, how much revenue we were generating, despite not getting commission reports from our partners for weeks or months. And we were able to attribute revenues to all our marketing activities right down to the click. I think that's what gave us the edge because our competitors weren't able to do this. They just knew which advertising campaigns were profitable rather than understanding which elements of their campaigns were working. That resulted in a lot of cash being thrown away.

PART 2

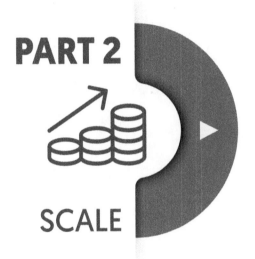

SCALE

3

Scale-up Leadership

By now you're three or four years into your business, and things are falling into place. You've established a team of people to help you run it – maybe there are a dozen of you. You have a solid set of customers, with more coming on board all the time. And you're starting to feel confident that maybe, just maybe, you might be able to sell this enterprise in a few years' time. If you've reached that point, congratulations. Most businesses don't manage to survive their first year, let alone evolve into something that resembles a viable company. You've achieved a lot.

And yet... I hate to burst your bubble, but you're about to enter your toughest period so far. The main purpose of the scale-up period is to prepare for your eventual sale and exit, which means you learning to see your business in a different way. You're not living hand to mouth like you were when you started up, but you do have to undergo a personal transformation the like of which you've never experienced before.

This involves morphing from being the founder who dives in and troubleshoots all the time to being the person who trusts their employees to do it for them. To achieve this, you have to recruit people who will eventually be capable of running your business without you because one day they will do just that. What's more, to support them in their work and to give you oversight and control, you need systems and processes for everyone to work with. And to top it off, you must inspire your people to work together to achieve your vision for the business. In other words, you have to become a leader.

This is important for two reasons:

↗ It enables your business to keep growing. If you remain the key decision-maker and problem-solver, your company will never become bigger than you – it will always be defined by your personal strengths and weaknesses.

↗ You'll increase your chances of walking away from it with full cash, rather than having to stay on after you've sold. Because when you receive an expression of interest from a buyer, they'll want to be confident that your company isn't dependent on you for its functioning. If you only start pulling together a set of people who can run it shortly before you sell, your acquirer will insist that you stay on for several years afterwards and will only pay you the full amount when you complete certain milestones. This is called an earn-out, and it's why you need to put a high-performing senior management team in place in the scale-up phase – and to lead it well.

Here's the challenge. If you're anything like me, you're the kind of entrepreneur who loves coming up with ideas and solving problems on the fly – it's likely to be what's enabled you to build your business successfully so far. But what's probably more alien to you is delegating, creating systems and processes, and managing your company as an entity outside of yourself. If you've had leadership experience in previous roles it might be easier for you, but unless you've already run a 50+ person business it's hard to understand what it takes to lead that many people effectively. And a lack of leadership is the main reason why so few companies scale successfully. So if you're feeling a bit mystified as to why your business isn't growing as quickly as it did in the beginning, it could be because you haven't adapted to the different approach you need to take.

I can't tell you how excruciatingly painful I found this transition into leadership to be. Personal change is the hardest thing in the world, but if you don't evolve as an individual you'll hold your company back. What got you from start-up to scale-up won't get you from scale-up to exit; it requires a different mindset and a new set of skills. When you're achieving your vision and goals through other people, it can feel incredibly frustrating. This can blindside you if you're not careful, so you do need to grow your mind as well as your turnover.

How it works

A classic example of why a leadership approach is crucial is in your relationship with your customers. You've probably developed a close personal relationship with the ones that you've had from the early days.

They might expect that it will carry on as you grow, but when you're a scale-up you can't possibly meet all their demands yourself. You can't just answer an email from a customer and say, 'Yes, no problem – we'll get on to it next week.' Now that you have a customer service team, it needs to know that it's trusted to handle this kind of thing. This team in turn should have a change request process to ensure that any changes are viable for the business and can be managed efficiently. Nor should you be the main recruiter of new customers – you have a head of sales for that. It's all bigger than you.

This is important because it makes business acquirers nervous if the founder of a company is the same person who brings in most of the customers and to whom customers turn if there's a problem. They wonder what would happen if you were to leave after they've bought your business. Would your customers depart as well? You should have dedicated teams to look after existing customers and bring in new ones; otherwise you'll be unlikely to monetise all your investment without an earn-out.

Learning is everything

My MBA research showed me that the most successful companies were those run by people who never stop learning. This told me that I needed to grow into my new role in a deliberate way rather than just picking up knowledge as I went along. I had to get out of the 'weeds' of my business and give myself space to discover new things.

So I worked with coaches and mentors who

supported me on my journey, went on several director courses at the Institute of Directors and read a huge amount about leadership. I also joined clubs in London (such as HELM) where I could meet other entrepreneurs in similar businesses and networked with them to share experiences. I was hungry to learn what it meant to be a leader rather than a founder, so that I could be the powering force behind my business and grow it as quickly as possible.

One of my major challenges was learning to trust my people and delegate without micromanaging them. Putting in place a high-quality leadership team helped with that, as did having a system of KPIs to measure progress. But it was psychologically painful for me to take a step back from my company. I think this mindset went back to my childhood; if I wanted something I had to work for it myself, and if something needed to be done I had to do it. I didn't always know how, but I learned and got on with it. This sheer determination served me well when I started all my businesses, but it was only in my most recent one, Smart Apprentices, that I grew into being a leader. It wasn't an easy transition, and neither will it be for you. You're morphing from a caterpillar into a butterfly, and there's no avoiding the messy phase in the middle.

It gets easier

If this all sounds a bit off-putting, let me reassure you that it gets less painful as you progress through the scale-up phase. Running a young business is chaotic and stressful but if you can get your structure, processes and leadership team in place with the right people, you'll find that your time is freed up and you can start to have fun again. You'll have space to explore new interests (maybe in preparation for the exit) and you can also pick and choose which areas of the business you want to spend most time on.

My choice was the visionary area. Having learned bitter lessons from the collapse of my first business, I made sure that I constantly looked to the wider world – competitors, market trends and political changes – so that I could see what was coming over the horizon. This is something that you can never delegate as a leader, and is just one example of how you still add enormous value to your business even when you've taken more of a back seat.

Eventually you'll start to see your business not as your alter ego but as an entity that you lead and manage. It's not an extension of you any longer, but something that will grow way bigger than you and one day pay you a handsome return. What's more, towards the end of the scale-up phase you'll be planning your succession, which could mean bringing in somebody as managing director. This is still two or three years away, but it's worth bearing in mind when you feel that your personal transformation is a struggle.

The strategic importance of your senior leadership team

When I ran my first business, Start-Right, I didn't even know what a leadership team was. I spent my time scheduling client calls and even buying toilet rolls and coffee when they ran out. This clouded the bigger picture for me; I was running around looking after the details instead of discovering that our market was about to implode. So it's critical to recruit and develop your senior leadership team as quickly as you can. Don't wait until you 'need' it.

What's more, if your intention is to sell and exit your business at the same time, you need to make yourself dispensable from early on. You have to have people in it from the beginning who will stay with it after you've left and who are capable of running it without you. That was the secret of my ability to move away when I sold Smart Apprentices; I had a high-performing group of leaders who'd worked well together for many years and who had a track record of delivering. Two members had been with me from the start and the others from shortly after – they weren't parachuted in a couple of years before the end.

I brought in Danny, our sales director, from the word go; he was responsible for new business. My next early appointment was Andy, our IT director, and later Helen, who looked after our customer retention. All three were given equity, which not only incentivised them to grow the business but also helped to attract them to Smart Apprentices in the first place. This was especially important for Helen as she'd worked for a blue-chip software firm in London and was hugely experienced. I couldn't match her salary but the equity helped to fill the gap. Recruiting these people meant that we became a 'proper' business but I still wanted more expert input, so I appointed a board of non-executive directors to hold both myself and the management team to account. Once I had a board in place and a senior team working effectively, it made a significant difference to how free I was to leave the business when we eventually sold. This sounds as if it worked very neatly, but my plans were thrown into disarray when Helen decided to leave for personal reasons and I had to replace her. You always have to be ready for unexpected challenges.

My MBA research backs this up: all the owners of fast-growing businesses I interviewed said that it was their senior leadership team which had the highest impact on their growth. Without these critical people in place, you won't expand as quickly as you'd like because you'll be forever dealing with every issue yourself. Not only that, but your venture won't benefit from the skills, attitudes and diversity of employees who come from different backgrounds to you. That's why I recommend thinking big early on by seeking out the brightest and best to join you at a senior level.

If this seems a little daunting, it may be helpful to remember that you're not starting this senior team from scratch. If you've done your recruiting right in the start-up phase, you'll have people who are responsible for marketing, sales, finance, operations and product or technology. The main difference is that it was okay then to have one or two of these roles filled by external consultants or the odd freelancer. Now, however, you need feet on the ground. You should also have someone with HR expertise who can ensure consistency of employment contracts and working practices, and who can help to build the culture. It doesn't necessarily have to be a full-time role but it does need to be in-house.

Recruiting your senior team

In the start-up phase, even your senior people had an

overlap in their responsibilities. It's never 'not my job' when the company's survival is at stake. But now that you're formalising your HR structure, you need more long-term clarity in terms of roles and responsibilities.

Your first task is to identify what roles you have to fill. What are their characteristics? What work needs to be done? And are the people currently occupying them the most appropriate ones? Can they help you to achieve the growth you need during this critical period? Some of your early recruits may be suitable but some may not. It's tempting to leave them in their roles because none of us likes having difficult conversations about potential and performance, but I urge you not to. You need to look at the personalities, skills and experience that are required for each role and to tackle the problem before you need to. If somebody isn't right for the next stage, it's best to shift them to another job or move them out of the business altogether. That might sound harsh, but it's no fun for them to do work that isn't a good fit for them – it's stressful and demoralising. It's far better to prevent this from happening by making tough decisions early on.

Once you have your vacant seats identified, you can recruit people for them who are an excellent match in terms of the skills and characteristics required. You should also create job descriptions outlining the role, the responsibilities and the goals for each. Also, think about how you'll make those people accountable for their area of responsibility and what systems you'll use to measure this.

I'm often asked the best ways of attracting high-quality people into an unpredictable and insecure business.

The answer is: with difficulty. And yet you must have great leaders and managers if you're to grow as quickly as you want to, so you have to find a way. I've found that many experienced people who work in corporate jobs are looking for something more exciting and where they can make a direct impact. You may only have 15 people, but if you sell them the story of where you're going and what they'll be doing to get you there, it makes a huge difference.

You can also offer them share options or equity in your company. This helps you to avoid paying over and above market salary rates because the shares are effectively part of their remuneration. It's no bad thing in any case as it gives them the motivation to help you achieve a high valuation. And your eventual acquirer will want to see that your senior team is fully committed to the business through owning some of it.

Create a cohesive team

Getting the right people into the right roles is a bit like a jigsaw puzzle. For instance, in sales we had Danny, who headed up customer acquisition, and Helen, who headed up customer retention. Their temperaments were well suited to what they did; Danny had a 'hunter' mentality and loved the thrill of the chase, whereas Helen was a 'harvester' and was great at nurturing our customer relationships.

It's so important that you have the right mix of skills in your leadership team and also the right personalities. We brought in one person who was brilliant, but she was also a pain to work with. She was forever taking up people's time with her problems and would regularly throw her toys out of the pram when she didn't get her way. We made it work because I'd already employed her permanently, so we had no choice. But it wasn't the culture I wanted in my leadership team. Had I initially contracted with her for a three-month project instead, I might have been forewarned.

That's why I always prefer to 'try before I buy'. I've made the mistake of not doing this a few times, but now I avoid committing myself upfront if I can. For instance, I brought in someone who came with great references and was clearly an accomplished strategist, but the problem was that he couldn't get anything done. He theorised and talked a lot, and we had some beautiful PowerPoints and Gantt charts from him, but he couldn't get his sleeves rolled up to sort anything out. He just wasn't the right kind of person for a fast-growing enterprise. Although my hope had been for him to take us to exit, luckily I'd only contracted him for 90 days.

Managing your senior team

During your scale-up phase you'll gradually go from perhaps a dozen employees to 50, and this changes the nature of your business entirely. You can't oversee things personally anymore, so you need to ensure that everyone understands your vision and what they need to do to achieve it. That's okay because you have your senior team to handle things. Or is it? It can be tempting to become complacent at this stage; you have a great set of people, so why not take your foot off the pedal? If you're lucky you can, but for most of us it's not so simple. Even if you've done your best to select the right leaders, you won't always get it right first time – some of them won't perform. That means you can't afford to lose sight of what people are doing and how well they're performing, even for a week. Leadership is about steering the team in the right direction and making sure that they're all working together rather than veering off at different angles.

I'll go into more details about the systems and processes you can set up to manage this in the next chapter, but for now it's worth thinking about how you're going to encourage your team to cohere. Having fun is something that's easy to forget about when you're ultra-focused on growing your revenue, but it's important for everyone, not only your senior staff. Why do they come into work each day? And why do they work for *you*?

I believe that helping people to achieve their personal aspirations can be a major motivator for them to do a good job at work because you're treating them as a whole person rather than just an employee. Even prior to the Covid-19 pandemic we were a virtual company, with most people working from home, so we worked hard to create a sense of community. Every three months we'd come together in person. We'd spend the morning on personal development, bringing in a personal trainer to help people with their fitness goals, for instance. Or we might devote the time to training; for example, we invited a barrister to talk to us about conflict resolution, which was an eye-opener for us all. Then in the afternoon we'd go and have some fun; we'd play games, go for walks and ice cream – that kind of thing.

We also brought this approach into our weekly

Friday morning video calls, which the whole company would attend. We'd sometimes have a comedian to tell jokes and get everybody laughing or we'd ask people to share their success stories outside of work. It might be that one person's son had received great exam results or that someone else had finally managed to house train their puppy. Of course, we'd celebrate business successes too. When everyone knows that the half-year target has been achieved, it doesn't seem so hard to reach the final goal.

As CEO you can get sucked into a tunnel vision of working towards your exit, but you have to remember that not everybody is like you. Even your leadership team doesn't have the same focus, let alone your UX designers and other staff. I always tried to make our communications about more than just money. Even when I did talk about revenue, it would be in terms of how good financials would enable us to do more exciting things within the business.

People issues

Each of your people might be fantastic individually, but if there's conflict between them it can be absolutely toxic for everyone and sabotage your business. This is particularly relevant to your leadership team. However careful you've been to set your culture, and to 'try before you buy' when you recruit people, you'll find that a good deal of your time will be spent sorting out people problems.

Suppose your platform has an outage and there's a massive upsurge in support tickets. Your head of operations is desperate to know the average response time, but your head of support would rather focus on servicing customers. The conflict reaches your desk. What do you do? Being the CEO of a scale-up business, you don't want to get sucked into day-to-day operational issues, but at the same time you know that you can't let this escalate.

First, you stay calm and listen. Often people only want to vent, so let them talk about their frustration and try not to come up with solutions before you know what the problem's really about. Be fair and hear both sides, then try to get them to work together to resolve things. That's easier said than done, but your role isn't to be a referee – it's to achieve a solution that works for all. In my experience most conflict comes from people not understanding each other, so if you can help them to see each other's points of view, that will stand you in good stead for the future as well.

Of course, the clearer your processes are, the easier it is to resolve arguments. If you have internal KPIs for what's reasonable to expect in terms of producing reports, for instance, then you have something to refer to. This is where it's different to when you were in the start-up phase. Then, everyone was more aligned with the core aims of the business, which helped people understand what they were supposed to be doing. Personal egos were more easily set aside. Now that you have a bigger team, people are further removed from those aims and you are too, so you have to be fair and apply the rules equally.

Conflicts can cause people to leave your business, so they need to be taken seriously. When arguments develop it can also be stressful for the rest of the leadership team. It can be very damaging when you have to performance manage someone, and be horribly unsettling both for you and for other people in your business.

Leading your business

Picture the scene. Your chief marketing officer has created a presentation to show to your most important customers and it focuses on a new feature that you've developed for your product. It's the first time that you've shown it to anyone, and if these customers buy into it, others will follow. All the resources that you've poured into creating the feature hinge on this one meeting, so you can't afford to mess it up. But when you pay your marketing person a visit a couple of days before the presentation to check how it's going, you're not impressed. The facts in it are correct but there's no pzazz or excitement and you can't imagine anyone wanting to buy it. This is a serious disappointment.

What do you do? If you were a start-up CEO you'd take the presentation and rewrite it yourself. You'd make sure it looked exactly as you wanted and if that involved overruling your marketing person, so be it. However, you're not a start-up CEO anymore; you're a *scale-up* CEO. You can't just roll up your sleeves and do somebody else's job for them; not only is it demotivating for them, but they won't learn from their mistakes. Instead, you have to find a way to explain what's wrong with the presentation so that they can fix it themselves.

Leading people involves developing them; it can be an incredibly frustrating process, especially when you're used to being hands-on all the time. I see it like teaching your children to tie their own shoelaces. It would be so much easier to do it for them so that you can get out of the door with no trouble. But then they'll never learn to do it for themselves. In the same way, your role is to support your team to achieve your vision for the business, and if that means taking the time to develop them, it's what you have to do.

Your culture

The parenting analogy follows through into creating your business culture because it comes from you – the head of the 'family'. If you're a parent you no doubt have certain expectations of how everyone behaves at home, and if you're not, you probably had one who did. It's the same with your business; it starts with your leadership team and follows through to every employee.

At Smart Apprentices our culture was based around being honest and getting things done. Yours might be different, but as the founder it's helpful if you talk about why you think your values are important, what your vision is and how you want people to work. You also have to walk your talk. For instance, something I encouraged was that if anyone saw something going on that they didn't think was right, they should call it out. That meant that when I came up with an idea somebody else thought was stupid, I had to listen to them. Similarly, I found it incredibly frustrating when people circled round an issue and waited for ages before sorting it out; I let people know that there was never an excuse for not getting things done. That meant that if one of my people came to me for help with something and I promised my support, I had to give it within the timescale I set. I couldn't expect everyone else to be honest and action oriented if I wasn't myself.

Towards the end of the scale-up phase we formalised our culture, and you might like to do that too. For instance, we subscribed to Investors in People for five years, which guided us in setting our vision and values. We inscribed these visions and values on posters and added them to our Zoom backgrounds and the backs of the brochures we gave out at our quarterly get-togethers. But far more effective than any poster was for me to talk about the culture and to live it. You can put whatever words you like on a wall – it doesn't mean that people will remember them. But when everyone has a personal experience of you making the culture real, it sticks.

Quick recap

- ↗ The purpose of the scale-up phase is to prepare the business for your eventual exit.
- ↗ You need to start seeing your business as something outside of yourself.
- ↗ A high-performing leadership team is essential.
- ↗ Your leadership skills are something that you must deliberately develop.
- ↗ Leadership means developing people rather than doing things for them.

Questions to ask yourself

- ↗ How do I see my business – as something that's part of me or as something that's outside of me?
- ↗ Am I ready to become a leader?
- ↗ What can I do to improve my leadership abilities?
- ↗ Who in my current team is capable of taking us to exit, and who isn't?
- ↗ Am I setting a company culture that will lead my business to success?

An Entrepreneur's Experience

Rob Hamilton

In 1999, after training as a chartered surveyor, Rob founded The Instant Group, a worldwide marketplace for companies wanting serviced offices. He grew the business organically, opened offices overseas and added new services, selling a significant stake to private equity in 2012. He sold the remainder in a secondary buyout in 2018, and the business was then sold to IWG for £320 million in 2022.

In 2012 Rob also founded Ride25, a round-the-world cycle adventure which has raised over £1 million for charity so far. In addition to that, he's an angel investor and non-executive director for various companies, including a venture capital firm called Love Ventures. His main love is getting businesses started and then scaling them.

I asked Rob to share with me the lessons he's learned about starting, scaling and selling a business. Here are some of the highlights.

If possible, avoid diluting your share of the business by taking external investment

When I first started Instant, the serviced office sector was looked down upon; various companies had gone bust, which meant that people didn't trust the economics of the model. So to gain funding, I asked the people who owned the small business I worked for at the time if they would invest. They ended up funding half of it, with the other half coming from my credit card. The total amount was £20,000, and that was the only outside capital I ever had. The £20,000 was put into the business as a loan and repaid within the first 18 months. From the outset I had the right to buy the shares that I didn't own for a set amount, but rather than doing this I reached an agreement with the original investors that they would have 4 per cent of the group.

I heavily incentivised people working in the company with shares, so by the time I sold it over 30 per cent was owned by them. However, I still owned the majority myself. Controlling so much of my business is why I've been able to do so many different things with it. And when I came to sell, I reaped the benefit. I think it's a shame now when founders end up with a small percentage of their companies. I know things are different from 20 years ago, but all the people who've generated real money have done so without lots of fundraising. There's no reason why that can't happen with today's start-ups.

If you're in difficulty, being transparent with your employees allows them to help you

When we opened in Australia and America, I was drawn in lots of different directions, and it was the one time that the business didn't grow. After two years of stalled figures, we were getting low on cash and were close to being unable to pay salaries. I had a conversation with my two MDs in which we agreed that we would be transparent with the whole company about the situation. We told everyone exactly where we were and presented our finances, cash and profitability figures. Then, my god, we had the most unlikely people bring in sales because everybody had to contribute. After that, I was always open and transparent with my employees.

Work out how the different elements of your business complement each other

Four years in with Instant, we recognised there were companies that wanted serviced offices for hundreds of people, not just for five or ten, which is the market we'd been serving so far. And nothing existed for them. So we created a new product for large corporates that needed offices for 500 people for three years. It was brilliant because it gave us medium-term contracts, fixed margins and fixed profitability; it was cash generative from day one. The two parts of the business also worked well together. The small business side was more like retail, with bumpy income but solid growth; this was attractive to private equity, which is what we sold to in the end.

If you don't want to do an earn-out, separate yourself from your business well before you sell

In 2011 we began to sell the business, primarily because I'd had enough of running it and was more interested in having variety in my life! So I recruited an external CEO to run it and lead a management buyout with private equity backing. It then took 12 months to get the business ready for sale and to complete the transaction. The business undoubtedly changed from being owner managed to private equity backed.

The exit isn't necessarily the end of your story

After the sale, I went through a three-year nightmare in which I was sued by the private equity firm which had bought my business. Within a few weeks it had fired many people in my team, and then it came after me with a warranty claim. Not something I would recommend, but it is something to be aware of when you sell up! It all ended well and I exited completely in 2018.

It's thousands of tiny improvements that create success, not necessarily one big one

At Instant it was always about managing the risks and changing and improving what we did, thousands and thousands of times. All those tiny changes made the business work – there was no one big thing. We just worked hard and kept on going. We were also fanatical about keeping our costs low right up until the end, which helped us to ride out the hard times. When we opened in America, for instance, we did it in a way that involved little capital and didn't recruit too many people; that way, when our losses came, they were manageable.

4

Scale-up Infrastructure

successful scale-up business is a bit like a sports team. There's a captain (that's you), there are players (your employees), there's a goal or objective for the game (your business target) and there are rules. It's the rules that I'm exploring in this chapter, because without them any game would fall into chaos. Players wouldn't know what to do, no one would know if they were winning or not, and with no time limit on the game there would be little sense of urgency. Rules bring people together and get them working productively towards a common aim; they provide resolutions for arguments and disputes and they allow the captain to focus on leading the team rather than getting involved in every kick or throw.

Systems and processes

Rules in your business take the form of systems and processes. They make it easier for you to separate yourself from the day-to-day running of your company because they give your people a way of aligning themselves to your vision without you always being by their side. It's as if you've partially replaced yourself with an infrastructure that not only supports your teams, but that also gives you an oversight of what's going on.

Much of this is about retaining a level of control to make up for your new arms-length leadership role. How can you check that someone's authorised to spend money on the company's behalf? You need a purchase order system with a sign-off process. What happens when someone calls in sick? You need an employee absence process. How can you be sure that company data is being safely handled? You need a data management process. And how can you be confident that people know how to use these processes and are committed to putting them into practice? You guessed it: you need an employee onboarding process which ensures that they know what to do.

But it's not only about control and support; it's also about making your company attractive to an eventual acquirer. If your business isn't highly organised and operationally competent in a way that doesn't rely on you, it will be seen as high risk. For this reason (and others) you also need to ensure that you're legally compliant. In the UK there's a lot of regulation, especially in the areas of data protection and human resources, and it's easy to inadvertently break the law. For instance, when you were a start-up it might have been fine for you to give flexible hours to one employee and not others, but now that you have a bank of staff you have to treat everyone the same. Otherwise you're laying yourself open to lawsuits, which is something that any potential acquirer will feel nervous about. The thing to remember is that some of these processes are difficult, if not impossible, to retrofit, so you need to build them in from early on. The devil is so often in the detail, which will be ruthlessly unpicked during the due diligence process by the business that acquires you.

Setting up processes isn't easy to do. I understand why because, like you, I've started companies from nothing and know that the default focus is on product, product, product and sales, sales, sales. What entrepreneur feels excited at the idea of systematising things? It's hardly the highlight of our day. And I'll be honest, it can sometimes be frustrating when you have to keep to the rules you've created – there's no more 'just buying' something for the business or 'just hiring' someone to fill a gap. You can't take shortcuts anymore; you have to set an example of how to work in a professional way.

It also felt overwhelming for me. I found myself wondering whether it was necessary to systematise a business that (at the time) consisted of only 15 people.

But I knew that I had to bite the bullet early on because while it's one thing to introduce systems to 15 people, it's another thing to do it to 50. It's far easier to put processes in place before you really need them than it is to leave it until it becomes a major operation. Overlooking the 'boring' stuff will come back to bite you later, when you have to stay on to run a company that you no longer own because it can't operate without you.

We looked at various models that we could use to help us put a structure in place and ended up implementing ISO 27001 to protect our technical compliance and ISO 9001 to protect our management and leadership compliance. The process was horrendously demanding as it involved us setting up frameworks and procedures for pretty much everything, but it did force us to become professionalised. We decided that we needed stronger procedures to cover the following areas:

↗ finance
↗ business performance
↗ people management
↗ data management
↗ commercial contracts.

Finance

It's important to have business metrics in place to keep tabs on your financial performance, especially given that you're trying to grow quickly. It's frighteningly easy to lose control of your cash flow and profit tracking when everything is moving fast. As your customer base increases you'll need to understand which of your customers, products and services are contributing most and least to your profit. For example, you may have a high-maintenance customer who absorbs a lot of your resources. This creates a missed opportunity cost: what else could you be doing while servicing that needy customer? Of course, you may choose to keep them if there's a bigger business reason for it, but it's a decision you should make with the facts to hand rather than basing it on emotion.

I can't stress enough how this means thinking like a big company from now on. Large corporations have cost centres as part of their expenditure budgeting and so should you. Do you know how much you're spending on travel, for instance? More importantly, can you relate part of your travel costs to specific customers or particular customer acquisitions? If you have the information, you can decide whether or not it's necessary. Also, don't assume that your spending will always rise: it should flex along with your business performance, which means reducing it if you don't hit your sales goals. If your revenue trajectory to exit is three years and midway through year two you're not on track, you should readjust your budgets – you can't spend what you haven't got.

Business performance

Your financial performance is clearly important, but it's retrospective. When you're aiming to grow quickly you can't wait until the end of the month to discover that you didn't do as well as you intended – you need forward visibility as well. That means putting in place systems and processes that alert you in real time as to whether you're in danger of not hitting your KPIs. I had a dashboard with a scorecard giving me top-level data, and I deliberately kept it simple because I find it hard to cope with lots of detail. It's something I've carried on into my new businesses. For instance, for my current fledgling recruitment business, all I want to know is how many new employers have created an opportunity; of those, how many have been liked; and of those likes, how many have been mutually liked. They're the KPIs that tell me how well my business is performing, and I can drill down to see more detail if I want to.

For you to create a similar dashboard involves being clear on the drivers for your business. Imagine that you're on a desert island, completely cut off from the world, and you're desperate to know how your company is doing. What would be the three or four KPIs that would tell you if it's on track to achieve its goals? Given that you're heading for an eventual exit, your KPIs should be the ones that are important for that. So link them to what you think your buyer will be most interested in. If you consider that market share will be more attractive to a potential acquirer than profitability, base your measurements on market share.

There's so much data washing around in any business that it's easy to be overwhelmed by it, so try and focus on the critical metrics and keep your head out of the weeds. If you need to, you can always dig down further after you've seen the big picture.

You can make this easier by investing in external systems. It was a big decision to bring in the CRM system Salesforce when we were only four years old, because it was expensive. Was it a sledgehammer to crack a nut, we wondered? But it more than paid for itself as we went through the scale-up phase because we could manipulate our customer data to see exactly what was going on. And it was particularly attractive to buyers to have access to this data when we came to sell.

People management

Until we could afford an internal HR person, we used the Investors in People accreditation to give us the framework for an HR structure. It helped us to realise that our key competitive advantage was our people, and that without the right ones we couldn't develop innovative technology, attractive marketing or excellent customer service. It also guided us to an understanding of what needs our employees had, so that they could deliver our business plan.

As well as creating development plans for our existing people, we also invested a lot of time and resources into formalising our selection and onboarding processes for new hires. The outcome of this was that we reduced the number of those who didn't make it past their probationary periods, increasing the length of time we retained our talent by 50 per cent. The Investors in People modelling also inspired us to create a staff handbook, which contained our company policies and expectations about how people should behave if they wanted to thrive in our company.

This focus on HR processes was important for two reasons: it reduced the need for me to be personally involved in recruiting junior staff, and it meant that we didn't have any legal axes hanging over our heads. For instance, one of our people who worked from home developed repetitive strain injury and claimed that she hadn't been told how to set up her PC. We had her signature on a document which stated that she'd received and actioned this information, which mitigated our liability. This is the sort of thing that your acquirer will want to see.

Something else to think about with your people management structures is who should oversee all your systems and processes. I knew that I wasn't systematic enough to do this – my role was to be the visionary who made sure that we were developing competitor-beating products that our customers would buy. So I made sure that a couple of people in my leadership team were the organised type. Ann and Helen came from large organisations and were used to working in a structured way, and they also had the right mentality for it, so they contributed hugely to how efficient and process driven we became.

Data management

I can't be alone in being amazed by the amount of data protection legislation that businesses have to comply with – it's hard to conceive of this when you first start up. Unfortunately, in law, ignorance isn't an excuse; you're expected to know about all the relevant regulations and comply with them in the same way a much larger organisation does. To ensure that we were doing this properly, we gave all our staff GDPR compliance training and assessments and kept on top of how they were processing our clients' data. It's a minefield, and so easy to do the wrong thing if you're not careful. For example, I didn't realise at first that anyone accessing the data of a minor (we had some users of our platform who were 16 or 17) had to go through a criminal records check. I'd assumed that it was only needed if they were to meet them in person.

As with HR legalities, it's not just about protecting your business from litigation, but about being attractive to a prospective buyer. You'll need to have all your data protection procedures watertight if they're to feel reassured that you don't represent a ticking bomb for them.

Commercial contracts

In the start-up phase, you're so keen to acquire new customers that it can be tempting to cut corners so you can get them over the line, leaving formal contracts to take a back seat. However, this approach will scupper you as you grow; it will certainly not stand up to scrutiny when you try to sell your company. Also, what would happen if your contact at the customer's company were promoted or decided to leave? You'd be vulnerable to the whims of their successor.

To counter this, you need to introduce the discipline of asking every customer to sign a contract or purchase order. I'll admit that this has its downsides – it can significantly lengthen the time it takes to bring them on board and can risk someone in higher authority questioning the order and taking it back to tender. It wasn't a popular move with my sales team, that's for sure. But I learned that without signed agreements it's difficult to resolve disputes amicably because there is no formal contract to refer to. It's better to be safe than sorry.

Fast-growth goals

A major difference between a business that grows quickly and one that doesn't is that it's run by someone who knows exactly what they want to achieve and by when. The scale-up phase is no exception to this, which means that you must have a crystal-clear vision of your end goal, so shiny and bright that you can almost touch it. If you didn't have this when you started, you can't do without it now. Because keeping your eye on the prize is the most effective way of stoking your motivation to keep growing rapidly and sustainably.

At Smart Apprentices my goal was to achieve lasting financial security for my family by selling my company for as much as I could achieve, and I was prepared to risk everything for that. I was absolutely determined to change the legacy of deprivation I was left as a child by giving security to my children. And I did it; my kids are the only ones in my extended family who've been to private schools and university and are mortgage free. What are your goals for your business and why do you have them? Are they ones that will keep you fired up for the long road ahead? When the buzz of the start-up years is behind you, but the satisfaction of the sale is not yet in sight, it can be a challenge to keep your sense of urgency alive. Goals make a massive difference to that.

Of course, having goals is great but you also need to make yourself accountable for them. If you miss your objectives in the scale-up phase, it's more difficult to recover than when you were a start-up because your revenues and costs are so much higher. That's why you have to raise your head from the day-to-day detail and look across the whole organisation; it's the only way that you'll see problems arising before they hit you. Time goes so quickly – you can't afford to lose a week here or there by not moving forward at pace. During our scale-up phase, my goal was to get the business to £5 million turnover. We struggled at £3 million and hung around that level for much longer than I wanted, but at least I had the journey mapped out and knew where we were at. It meant that my team and I could make decisions about how to improve the situation.

Your hierarchy of goals

The concept of goals is one that most entrepreneurs are familiar with, but it's how to use them in a way that motivates everyone in the business that matters. The reality is that your company goals will only generate growth if you create an unbreakable connection between them and the personal objectives of the people who deliver them. That's how you create value for exit. Let's look at the hierarchy of goals so you can see what I mean.

1. **Long-term and medium-term horizon goals (approximately five and three years respectively):** these are based on on specific KPIs such as revenue, margin, types of customer, rate of acquisition, product portfolio and customer value. Those that are most important to you will depend on your type of business; just remember to choose the ones that will help you to build the most value for exit.

2. **12-month goals:** these support your long-term horizon goals by being more detailed and realistic.

The achievement of your annual goals should take you a significant way towards meeting your medium-term horizon goals.

3. **90-day goals:** these define the tangible targets and outputs that you're looking for over a three-month period, and which if delivered will take you towards your 12-month goal. For instance, it could be that one of your 90-day goals is to create a certain amount of revenue, so you need to decide what will help you achieve that. Should you develop a new product for a specific market by the end of the quarter? Win two major customers? Or something else? In my experience, 90 days is a long enough time frame to achieve a significant amount, but it's not so long that you're tempted to take your eye off the ball.

4. **30-day goals:** next, break down your 90-day goals into 30-day chunks. What do you need to achieve in the next month that will take you closer to your 90-day goals? Would it be achieving a certain milestone for your product development, for instance, or creating a marketing campaign aimed at your new prospective customers?

5. **Seven-day goals:** these follow the same principle as 30-day goals, but are shorter-term still. What does the business need to do this week if it's to stand a chance of achieving its 30-day goals? The beauty of measuring these near-horizon objectives is that they tell you whether you're off track more quickly than if you wait until the end of the month. For example, you'll know whether you've hit testing and delivery targets for product development or signed off the right stage of your marketing campaign.

Knowing what you need to get done at each stage of the goal hierarchy is the key to having the outcome you want at the end of the period. What's the one thing you need to do today that means you'll reach your weekly targets? What's the one thing you need to achieve this week that means you'll reach your goals this month? What's the one thing you need to achieve this month that will put you in a good position to meet your goals this quarter? And so on. The more you can break down your goals, the more achievable they are and the more laser focused you are on your long-term horizon.

During the scale-up phase at Smart Apprentices, my long-term horizon goal was to exit for significantly more than a ten times multiple of £1.5 million profit. We worked out that we'd therefore need to reach a revenue level of £5 million in six years' time, which meant that our next one-year goal was to reach a revenue of £3.8 million. So we had to figure out how to increase our revenue from what we already had. What sales could come from existing customers? And which ones? Also, how much new business would we have to bring in?

We predicted, based on experience, that we'd probably gain £2.9 million out of the £3.8 from existing customers, but we had to take a likely churn rate of 5 per cent into account. Our client team therefore came up with a plan for how they could retain as many customers as possible by risk rating them in our CRM system and working out how to keep the highest-risk ones on board. This gave them a target to focus on when it came to creating their own goals within the client management team. Their chunkiest goal was their 90-day one, so they asked themselves how they could see the level of customer risk on a 90-day basis. This was broken down into monthly and weekly goals. For instance, one goal was that, at the weekly meeting, any variation to the risk register would be discussed. Another was that the team would step up their monthly visits to weekly for clients who were approaching the renewal option in their contracts.

So far so good, but even if our customer retention plans worked, we knew we still had a revenue gap of £900,000. The previous year we'd only brought in £400,000 of new business, so it would clearly be a stretch to make our target. If we didn't do anything different to last year, we would achieve the same results. Where was the extra £500,000 of revenue going to come from? Could we build a new product in 90 days that we'd sell to our existing customers as an upgrade? We probably could, but that would increase our tech spend. So how could we reduce spend elsewhere without putting customer satisfaction and acquisition at risk? These were important questions, which we knew to ask because we were aware of exactly what we needed to achieve.

Not all companies are as relentlessly focused on growth. One of our competitors, for instance, won an award, and I could see at once that it became a distraction for them. They talked about it at every opportunity and were still dining out on it three or four years later. It was quite funny to watch, and when the market shifted beneath them without them realising, it became clear that they'd allowed it to cloud their vision.

Getting things done

It sounds obvious, but today is the only day you can do anything. That's why it's important to control your day rather than allowing it to control you. If you step in to support a colleague who's disorganised or if one of your team forgets to do something and it lands on your desk to deal with, you can get distracted. But when you know the *one* thing you must get done today, it makes achieving it easier. At Smart Apprentices I made it clear that there was never any excuse for anyone (including myself) not to tick off their one essential daily task, and it made a massive difference to what we got done each week.

Something that helped was to encourage people to take a 'power hour' when they needed to. They'd shut down all their tech and put their phone away so that they could concentrate solely on a task. We entrepreneurs are easy to distract because we get excited about every aspect of our businesses, but I found this a useful technique. If people can't last an hour without being able to get hold of you, there's something wrong.

I also love making goals visible. Before I finish for

the day, I write down what I need to do tomorrow and I underline the essential task. Sometimes I put it on a sticky note. My team used to laugh at all the little signs around my desk; I still have some of them now. Whatever helps you to remember your aim for the day is a good thing! Another way we made goals visible was to share what we'd achieved that day and what we were planning to achieve the next by posting them on the Basecamp collaboration platform.

Make your goals financial

There are all sorts of goals you could set, but it's best to choose concrete financial ones. In the scale-up phase it's all about growing your revenue, and numbers don't lie; you've either achieved your target at the end of the month or you haven't. It sounds mercenary, but if you allow yourself wriggle room by having a goal of 'creating a strong brand', for example, you'll find it easier not to hold yourself to account.

Another reason why financial goals are helpful is that the goal-setting around them sets the requirements for all other parts of the business: HR, resource planning, cost plans, product development, marketing and business development. If your revenue target dictates that you must invest in product development, you'll need to bring in more specialist people. Maybe you'll also need to train them and allocate extra office space. In addition, marketing spend might be needed, as well as a company-wide emphasis on new customer acquisition. It all comes from your financial goals.

You may have noticed that I've talked about your exit goal in terms of profit, but all your other goals in terms of revenue. That's because your company's value when you come to sell will almost certainly be based on a multiple of your profit, so you need to have a profit goal to aim at. However, buyers only look at your last three years of profits; they also want to see a long-term revenue growth trajectory that convinces them there's further for your business to go. So during the scale-up period your attention is best placed on investing whatever you need to grow your revenue – you can worry about profit later. That's not to say you should abandon all attempts to control your costs – if one expense goes up another must come down. There was never a year in our ten-year lifespan that we didn't return a profit, and retaining profit to invest in future growth was critical to our exit value. It's just that right now, your focus should be on what you need to spend in order to reach your revenue goals most quickly, while still remaining profitable.

Personal goals

If financial goals are king, personal goals are queen. When you're growing in the busy scale-up years, you might be tripling in size. So you have to bring people along with you, and one way to inspire them to perform at their best is to help them feel as if they're part of something larger than themselves. That's why we had our quarterly get-togethers, during which I encouraged everyone to set personal goals as well as work-related ones. The personal goals could be to do with anything – fitness, family, hobbies, reading; we didn't track them like we did with company goals but we did review them at our meet-ups. This was a way of treating our staff as if they were whole people, not just employees who did a job.

Your wellbeing

The notion of being a whole person leads to the topic of your wellbeing. The sheer weight of responsibility of being at the helm of a fast-growing business can feel overwhelming. Your employee numbers are shooting up, your costs are growing and you're grappling with how to lead your people through this challenging phase. It doesn't help that any mistakes you make now have a deep impact; a poor hire decision, for instance, can knock you sideways. For me, the biggest stress was that I wasn't playing to my strengths because I couldn't just dive in and innovate anymore. I was constantly asking myself, 'Have I made the right decision to do this? Who am I to lead this company? How am I going to manage it all?'

It can feel lonely, too. At the start-up stage you're a little team of bandits, all in it together. But now you're leading an organisation you can't offload your worries onto your people. You're not going to share how much you're struggling to learn new skills because you have to be the main person they can trust and have confidence in. They need to think that you know what you're doing, even if on some days you have little faith that you do.

It helps if you're fortunate enough to have family or close friends to confide in, and it's good to remember that advisors and coaches can offer professional support. Also, recognise that this is a big responsibility and you're doing the best you can. Most businesses never reach this stage, and even the ones that do don't all succeed. When you think of it like that, you're a bit of a hero.

Also, why not use the fact that you have a senior team running the show to take a holiday every now and then? Even buy a few luxuries that you couldn't afford when you were starting up? This will not only ease the stress, but it will also remind you why you started your business in the first place – to build the life you want.

And finally, see this as yet another reason to get some sound systems and processes set up. When you have clear visibility of your goals, your outputs and your achievements, you can manage the scale-up phase more easily – you can't do it without an infrastructure. The sooner you can see when you're going off track, the sooner you can do something about it and the less stressful the problem is to solve. It's when you leave things until they've become too big to deal with that panic sets in because you have nowhere else to go.

Quick recap

- ↗ If you're to separate yourself from the day-to-day running of your business, you need robust systems and processes.
- ↗ These keep your people aligned with your company's goals.
- ↗ They also help your business to grow quickly and to make it attractive to an eventual buyer.
- ↗ Create long-term financial goals that cascade down into shorter-term objectives for everyone to follow.
- ↗ This will help you to feel less stressed and more in control.

Questions to ask yourself

- ↗ What systems and processes do I have already?
- ↗ What would a potential buyer think of them?
- ↗ Are our company goals geared towards the exit?
- ↗ Does every single person in my business know what they need to achieve every week, month and quarter?
- ↗ Do I have a forward-looking system for anticipating problems before they arise?
- ↗ Am I looking after myself in all this?

An Entrepreneur's Experience

Alison Cooper

As an entrepreneur and innovator, Alison finds creative solutions to gaps in the market. She's founded and scaled multi-million-pound global businesses, including on-board food solution company En Route International, luxury holiday rental business Boutique Holiday Lets, design company Design'd Living and a language school in Germany. Having sold En Route in 2017, she branched into a new sector, founding jewellery brand Alicia J Diamonds. She noticed that young men who wanted high-quality engagement rings didn't know where to start or who to trust. The company is run by diamond experts and offers an approachable service, personally selling engagement rings and bespoke jewellery.

I asked Alison to share with me the lessons she's learned about starting, scaling and selling a business. Here are some of the highlights.

Before you launch a business, do your market research

I used to live in Germany and did a lot of motorway travelling, and noticed that service station food there was disappointing; they'd have dried bread rolls with a burger inside wrapped in loose cling film on the counter. I'd come from Britain where the M&S-style sandwich offering was just taking off and thought that I could sell pre-packaged sandwiches in Germany. I found a manufacturer and got on with it.

However, what I learned was that you can't take a product that is hugely successful in one country and simply drop it into another country without proper market research. It wasn't until I carried out the research that I discovered, for instance, that on German trains it was only elderly people with dentures who bought my sandwiches! German snacking products were based on crunchy rolls or baguettes, not soft bread – it was too unfamiliar for them. Also, Germans were ahead of the British in demanding no preservatives in their food, and environmentally friendly packaging. I was naive and also ahead of my time; the UK had an efficient chilled distribution network but Germany didn't yet have that infrastructure in place. The business actually led to me helping set that infrastructure up in Germany, but I learned a lot about researching your customer base before you begin.

Use every opportunity you can to learn

I lost my sandwich clients overnight when the BSE crisis struck and trade with Europe was stopped in its tracks, but I gained consultancy work. One project was helping catering company Compass UK and its subsidiary Eurest to bring branded food products from the likes of Upper Crust and Ritazza into the German corporate restaurants. I learned a lot about the bakery industry and who the big-plant bakers were. Watching the trucks that came into the UK every week for Upper Crust full of lovely baguettes inspired me. I thought that I could improve how bread was handled in the airline industry, and this became my next business.

As you scale, keep your focus on your core business and your culture

At En Route International, my aviation on-board solution business, we started with bakery products, but our clients soon wanted us to supply other types of food. We ended up providing cheese boards for Emirates and diversified into different product categories with varying temperature control requirements. We grew very fast, and I had to recruit quickly to keep up. I knew that I wanted to keep an eye on the culture of my business, which was difficult while we were expanding fast. There were some team members who came in at that time who didn't work out. I'd always advise having a three to six-month probation period, so that if things aren't right for either party, there's a way out.

During this scaling phase, we grew from £14 to over £40 million. In retrospect, I'd have stuck to our core product for longer. The expansion into new foods meant a whole new system of moving to shelf-chilled delivery from frozen delivered, which also meant a whole new warehouse and distribution system was needed.

When you don't own shares in your business anymore, it's hard to feel motivated

Scaling a business needs cash. Don't stick to just your industry when looking for investment. I fell into the trap of thinking that I couldn't get money from anywhere except banks. A lesson I learned is that there are many other investment avenues, such as family offices, venture capitalists, private equity, incubators, accelerators, even crowdfunding (although that wasn't really an option at the time).

These days many of these routes are more accessible to

business owners than they were to me at the time. I suggest getting in a specialist independent advisor to help – raising funds can be complex. Just because it's your business, you do not have to do it all yourself.

Part of the job of an independent advisor will be to help you prepare the right pitch. They should challenge your assumptions and help you anticipate questions. And of course, they will have expertise in working out the complexities of the deal itself.

Another option is to use invoice finance, suitable for B2B businesses. This is a method of relieving a cash flow problem, where you sell your invoices to a finance company and get paid a percentage straightaway, which removes your cash flow crisis.

One difficulty of raising investment is giving up a chunk of what you own. Try and hold on to as much share capital as you can – that's your worth. Challenge your thinking: do you give equity away for funding or do you do debt funding to prevent yourself from giving away your precious equity?

Lastly, pay close attention to choosing an investor for your company. Find someone who is in alignment with you, your business and your vision, as they will very much be someone you talk to and who will support you – it can be a lonely journey otherwise.

It's important to be hard working and resilient, but also to be kind to yourself and others

I'm a very determined person; like most entrepreneurs I'm at my best on high energy, thinking up new ideas. I love a challenge and I never think that something is impossible. But there will always be days when you're running a business when things go wrong and you're pushed to your limits. It's okay to show that you're vulnerable during those points. Don't be frightened to be honest about them. Take yourself out of the situation and have a breather.

Having time for people and being kind to them has been important to me on my journey. At En Route I'd always start the day by saying hello to everybody on both floors. I could see from people's faces whether something was up with them, and I could sense if there was a bad atmosphere in the department. Even though I was incredibly busy, with 82 staff and offices in America, Dubai, the UK and Australia, I'd always make time for people. Emotional intelligence has been a significant part of my success.

5

Scale-up Growth

Much of the scale-up phase revolves around learning to think like an eventual buyer of your company. What would they want to see? As we've covered, a high-performing leadership team and a rigorous set of systems and processes are two key elements. But there's a third, which is growth. In the scale-up phase your purpose is always to be growing because an acquirer will want to see that there's plenty of potential for more in the future. They love nothing better than a nice upward line on your revenue chart which shows no sign of levelling off. So you need to keep winning customers while also selling more of your products to the ones you already have.

And yet, despite the fact that you've probably been growing with a vengeance for a while now, many companies hit a wall once they mature into scale-up businesses. Smart Apprentices certainly did – I spent a lot of time trying to keep our trajectory on the upward curve. We also developed a product for a new market segment which took longer than I expected to gain traction, so I chose to delay my exit by a couple of years to focus on increasing the revenue from it.

If you're finding growing your sales to new and existing customers to be a problem, it's probably caused by two things:

↗ Your competitors have worked out what your competitive advantage is and are starting to copy you.
↗ You've already picked the low-hanging fruit, and your chosen market isn't large enough for you to make further inroads with your existing product.

Let's explore how you can deal with this.

Your product, market and competitors

When you were a start-up, you probably found it easy to fly under your competitors' radars – maybe that was even part of the fun. But now you're doing well, you'll have attracted some attention. It's not surprising – you've entered a growing market, one which you can create good revenue from, so you're bound to have rattled a few cages. In addition to that, you may be finding that new competitors are popping up with worrying frequency. This certainly happened to us, and was an inevitable consequence of us creating waves in a sector that had previously not been well served by fresh and innovative products. The main point is that, four or five years after your launch, your market is not the same as it was. You only get to have a competitive advantage for a short while, so you have to keep one step ahead if you're to maintain a strong position.

How do you keep growing when you have competitors snapping at your heels? It can be tempting to reduce your prices to increase your market share, but that's expensive and a dangerously short-term solution. It only takes one competitor to price-match or undercut you and you'll be leading a race to the bottom. Another option is to increase your marketing spend so that more customers are attracted to you, but there's a cost to that as well. Yet another is to enter a new market, but that's really hard. You'll be an unknown entity competing with businesses which already have a foothold there, and you'll have to spend a lot of money to overcome this.

These were the issues we faced at Smart Apprentices. We'd gained great traction during our start-up phase and by early in our scale-up period had achieved a 50 per cent share in our chosen segment – a huge slice. But then we stalled for a while. This forced us to think hard. It was clear to us that our customers were buying other online apprentice learning solutions, so what were they? Could we develop a product that was more innovative and better than what they were currently spending their budgets on? We felt that we could, and we also knew that if we could integrate it into our existing platform we'd have a distinct advantage because our customers would only have one dashboard and set of data to use.

So we researched the options and came up with three new product ideas. One of them was an online English and maths assessment tool for learners in these subjects. The company that currently made this product was highly profitable, so we knew that there was potential for us to take some of their market share. Of course, to entice customers away from the other provider we'd have to create something that was signif-icantly better than, and different to, theirs. In the end it wasn't as hard as we thought, and the product allowed us to take a greater share of our customers' wallets. It seemed like such an obvious idea, we wondered why we'd not thought of it before.

There are, however, a few things to watch out for if you're doing this yourself.

It's all about problem-solving

Just like when you developed your initial product, you have to think of your complementary product as solving a painful problem better than anyone else is doing. People will pay for that, but they won't pay for something that's not a big deal to them or that isn't a significant improvement on what's already there.

The problem we identified was that colleges needed to have a streamlined way of assessing learners' knowledge of English and maths, as this was a mandatory component for all apprentices, but that they also had other areas to assess their knowledge on as well. This was a headache for assessors, which we eased by making our solution flexible enough for them to extend to these other topics. Not only did this give them a more user-friendly way of assessing people, it also meant that they could reduce the number of platforms they used, giving them an end-to-end digital learning journey on one system. The icing on the cake was that our interface had a design that was way fresher than our competitor's, which had the appearance of something that had been created purely for the education market.

Always be innovative

To enter an aligned segment, you have to be creative

and to make something that's different to what's out there already. This isn't as hard as it may seem. I've found that, in technology, it's easier to be more innovative than it is to be faster or cheaper. If you've developed something distinctive and new, you'll find it's quicker to gain people's attention for it than if all you can talk about is price. Different will always win over fast and cheap.

Don't just add features

A common trap to fall into is to assume that, if you add new features to your existing product, you can charge more for it. While feature development is often necessary, it's rarely enough to transform your sales. For a start, it doesn't enable you to stand out with a fresh offering in the way that developing a new product can do. And second, it doesn't represent as much value to your customers. New features can be helpful at times, but they have a habit of getting lost in the marketing noise.

Maintain your margin

It's easy to increase revenue, but not so easy to increase your profit margin at the same time. In fact, your revenue can double, but if you're only receiving 2 per cent of the margin you're not much better off than you were before. While revenue is more important than short-term profit during the scale-up phase, profit is still a factor to consider or you'll be at risk of running out of cash and going out of business.

In summary, when you're scaling, upselling a new product to your existing customers is one of the easiest ways to grow because you don't have to win over a new audience and you can still increase your income. Of course, it may not be possible for you to do this – it depends on your product and market. But I'd be surprised if there were no opportunities for you to take a larger share of your customers' wallets – it just takes some lateral thinking.

Marketing the scale-up way

What's different about marketing a scale-up business to a start-up business? In some ways nothing, and in other ways everything. The things that should stay the same are your key marketing messages and the communication channels you use to put them out there. That's because by the time you reach this stage you should have tested and measured your messages and channels already. Unless something fundamental shifts in your market, such as a competitor responding in an aggressive way, stick to your guns. The start-up stage is when you trial and pivot; the scale-up stage is when you've nailed what you're doing and are committed to continuing with it.

I know how tempting it can be to keep changing things, especially if you're finding it hard to gain traction in your market. 'Surely it would be worth trying that new social media channel or refreshing our logo,' you think. But you already have your proof points – you know what works and what doesn't. Boredom with the status quo and a never-ending desire to tinker are the hallmarks of any entrepreneur, but you have to resist them because they distract you from what's important.

We fell into this trap at Smart Apprentices. During

our scale-up phase we signed with a digital marketing agency to test pay-per-click advertising on various social platforms. I don't know why we thought it was a good idea, because we hadn't worked with this agency before and our sales were still going up. It was probably because it was the shiny new thing at the time, and we felt we'd be missing out if we didn't give it a go. However, it was a painful process and we wasted a lot of time and money, even though the agency was first class. We ended up coming to the conclusion that the channels we were advertising on weren't suitable for a business-to-business company like ours; in fact, we were promoting ourselves to completely the wrong people.

So stick to your tried and tested key messages and your existing brand. You can trial and measure new channels as they appear, but only allocate a small amount of time and resources to exploring the potential of them. Retreat quickly if the results aren't what you hoped for. And bear in mind that even though the channel may be new, your messaging and marketing narrative has to be consistent with what you're putting out elsewhere. For instance, we slowly shifted away from online marketing towards offline, with events and webinars becoming increasingly important to us, but our messages were the same as before. Don't change your marketing for the sake of it.

Two markets

This is where marketing as a scale-up is different to when you were a start-up. Now that you have a solid customer base, you have two marketing tasks: continuing to gain new customers and growing the ones you have. As new competitors enter your market, you need to keep reassuring your existing customers that they've chosen the best solution to their problem. The last thing you want is for them to jump ship and for your hard work in attracting them to be wasted.

At Smart Apprentices we took this seriously. Because the people who bought our platform were different to the ones who used it, we had to make sure that our users were delighted with their experience. The challenge we faced was that our Smart Rooms technology saved colleges money by enabling video assessments, rather than assessors having to travel to see apprentices, but some were a bit stuck in their ways and didn't want to work remotely. So a person at the top would sign off this shiny new thing because they understood the money-saving potential, but users weren't helping them to reap the benefit. There was a risk that, when it came to budget review time, Smart Apprentices would be seen as an unnecessary luxury.

To address this we made a concerted effort to train and educate our users, and to motivate them to feel loyal to our system. We put on client events and webinars and created a User Academy. To incentivise users to get involved, we gave them three levels of accreditation – bronze, silver and gold – to reflect their knowledge of the platform. We even created 'champions' who received special privileges, such as access to early product releases and the opportunity to influence product enhancements. On top of that, we ramped up our storytelling around users in our social media, highlighting the successes that people were having with our system.

It's easy during the scale-up phase to carry on with the 'sell, sell, sell' approach of the early years, forgetting to retain the customers you already have. The thrill of the chase is addictive, after all. So it's important to split your marketing between your two key tasks – acquisition and retention – and to protect your retention spend, even though it might not be the most exciting element to you. If you don't do this, you'll end up with a leaky bucket where you lose as much revenue as you gain – a common problem during this period, and one which we absolutely nailed.

Scale-up finance

I've talked already about the fact that the scale-up phase is more about revenue than profit. In this period, you need to invest in what's going to deliver continued revenue and growth, not just this year but next year and the years after that.

However, unless you're happy to take external investment, staying in the black is absolutely essential. You're not looking to make the increase of profits your key driver (yet), but you are looking to at least generate some. It's true that your buyer will only look at your last three years' profits, but it's difficult to lift yourself from making a loss to making enough of a profit to generate a high exit value.

New revenue models

When we started we sold access to our platform via annual licences, which helped our cash flow enormously because all our customers paid yearly in advance. This was an innovation in our market as most of our competitors charged on a per licence basis; once their customers had used up the licences, they'd buy more. The downside of that was the lumpy revenue it brought in. We changed all that and were the first to use an annual subscription model.

However, it's during this period that you might want to look at alternative revenue models. By introducing 'annual renewable revenue', otherwise known as a subscription service, we didn't have to keep making one-off sales. We knew that one-off sales wouldn't be attractive to an acquirer and were hard work for us as well. The challenge this gave us, though, was that we had to keep a relentless focus on growing our subscriptions because if our sales flatlined one year it would have a negative impact on our growth the following year.

Funding and spending

Naturally you need to invest more as you grow, but remember that you also have more revenue coming in than you did before. We were fortunate enough to fund our growth through retained earnings, or our 'war chest' as I called it. We never had a year when we weren't profitable – why be in business if you're not making money? I've never seen the point of that. Sometimes we had to dip into our reserves to be able to keep investing in new product development and marketing, but that's what it was for – to drive our growth. It didn't mean that we had to lose money at any point.

During this period, I finally figured out business isn't that complicated. It feels painful at times, but all it involves is selling something for more than it costs you. Once you figure that out and start bringing in growing amounts of revenue, you'll be able to put some in the piggy bank as well. It's different for each business, but if you keep your exit in mind you'll find your own sweet spot. You're only spending what you need to achieve your end goal, on the things that will help you to grow your business. As your business grows, so does your revenue.

You may be wondering what happens if your business model means offering a service for free and finding ways to monetise it once you've gained some traction. My advice would be not to use that model. I've never offered anything for free – even a trial – because it's so hard to convert a freemium customer into a paid subscriber. It's far better to create something amazing that people want to buy.

Paying yourself

In your start-up phase you probably took the bare minimum out of the business to pay yourself because it wasn't there to take. But in the scale-up phase it is. During years four to seven at Smart Apprentices, the minimum we ever had in our reserve bank account was £1 million, and because I was the majority shareholder it was my decision whether to pay myself some of that money or reinvest it in the business. This is where your share structure can affect how you reward yourself during this period. For instance, if you have an investor or a co-founder who expects an early financial return, this can cause problems. In terms of personal reward, it's important to be on the same page as the people who have a stake in your company.

Generally, paying yourself gets easier during scale-up. When we first launched, I couldn't afford luxuries such as gym membership and holidays, and I didn't have time for them in any case. But after a few years I was able to take a lot more personal income out of the business. Not only was this good for my wellbeing, but it was also important that I was seen to be taking a good salary because I knew that I didn't want to stay on after exit. I wanted our eventual buyer to feel reassured that they wouldn't have to find the money for my replacement from other funds.

My salary towards the end of the scale-up phase was over £100,000 a year, but I was still relatively frugal about it. For instance, I'd switched to an interest-only mortgage on my house when we first launched, to reduce my outgoings. By scale-up we had enough money in the bank for me to take out a dividend which would have repaid my mortgage, but I didn't do that because I knew the funds would be cheaper if I took them at exit instead. At that point I'd pay 20 per cent capital gains tax, rather than the 38 per cent dividend tax I'd have paid earlier on. Also, I wanted to use the money to invest in the new product development that would get me to the end goal more quickly. That was far more worthwhile.

Finally, remember to keep a contingency fund during scale-up to cater for the unexpected. It could be a change to legislation that you can't control, or you might spot a lucrative opportunity that requires investment. Nobody saw Covid-19 coming, did they? I always made sure that we had at least three months' overhead in reserve in case we needed it. And if you can't do that? You'll have to use other people's money, which isn't ideal. But the real question to ask yourself is why you've not been able to charge enough for your product or control your costs sufficiently to create a contingency from your retained earnings. This is where a continuous stream of revenue and profit comes into its own.

Quick recap

- ↗ Growing your revenue is essential if you're to attract an eventual buyer.
- ↗ Creating a complementary product to your original one can help you to increase your sales.
- ↗ Don't change your marketing strategy just because you're growing.
- ↗ Spend at least as much time and money on retaining existing customers as on gaining new ones.
- ↗ Gear your finance management towards maximising sales and building a contingency fund.

Questions to ask yourself

- ↗ Are my sales continuing to grow, and if so, do they look likely to continue that way?
- ↗ How has the competitive landscape changed since we launched?
- ↗ What can we do to sell more of our product?
- ↗ Is there an opportunity to sell new products to the same market and customers?
- ↗ Are we doing enough to retain our existing customers?
- ↗ Am I paying myself the right amount, and in the right way, bearing in mind the exit?

An Entrepreneur's Experience

Chris Cole

For Chris it all began at the age of 16 with a sandwich delivery business, and when this quickly failed he went to college. After working at Johnson & Johnson to learn about sales and marketing, in 1997 he joined the team that launched Hydrogen, a radically different recruitment business. Over the following decade he invested in and grew Bionic, a business energy price comparison platform.

Along the way he's challenged himself and those around him, had a lot of fun and garnered awards such as the *Sunday Times* Best Company, Virgin Fast Track and Ernst and Young Entrepreneur. He's now the founder of 40 Fathoms, an investment company which funds start-up and scale-up businesses with teams that understand the importance of a unified culture and are hungry for success.

I asked Chris to share with me the lessons he's learned about starting, scaling and selling a business. Here are some of the highlights.

Start with the end in mind because it motivates you to learn

From the age of 11 I knew I wanted to run a business, and I remember thinking that I didn't have any money so it would need to be one with a low capital requirement. As I grew up, I realised that I needed to gain sales experience, which is why I joined Johnson & Johnson and also why I took sales jobs in shops as a kid. I was always pushing myself out of my comfort zone so that I could learn more. For instance,

I was offered two jobs in recruitment and I took the one in the smaller company because I thought I would learn more there.

A mentor who can share their experience is invaluable

I'd recommend to anyone starting a business that they find someone who has a bit of experience and can act as a mentor to help you shortcut some of your decisions. Our third partner at Hydrogen, Charles, did just that. When we first started I went to see him and he said, 'Well, why do you think your business is going to succeed?' And I said, 'I'm a really good recruiter. I know my trade.' 'That's not good enough,' he replied. 'You have to have a point of difference.' For a fairly cocky twenty-something like me that was a bit of a slap in the face, but it made me think.

Create points of difference and stick to them

This leads me to another lesson I learned, which is to know your point of difference. What's your right to trade? Back in the mid-1990s, London did not need another recruitment consultancy. So how could we stand out? We came up with three really simple things that almost seemed silly. The first was that we guaranteed our fees for six months, so if we placed someone in a job and they left before then, we'd give our client their money back. Clients loved that, as did candidates because they felt reassured that the placement would be right for them. The second was that we only put ourselves into markets where we could see there was a scarcity of candidates, and we didn't deviate from that. The third was that we treated people like we'd want our friends and relatives to be treated, doing things like making sure the candidates received feedback after going to interviews. It made both ethical and commercial sense.

Don't do everything yourself

I remember listening to Richard Branson years and years ago. He said, 'As soon as I find I'm doing something too much, I delegate it.' I chose, aged 29, to ignore that, and turned into the typical owner-manager, trying to do every job. Now I believe that you can get great talent to work for you, even if you're a young entrepreneur with little experience, as long as you have the right vision and values and the right opportunity to offer. If the person you recruit is any good, they will pay for themselves. When I look back on my career, I wonder how much time I spent working on the wrong things as opposed to thinking about where we were going and how the market was evolving. I should have been working on my business, not in it, and I wish I'd made that decision earlier.

Thank your customers and learn from them

Each time we placed a candidate I'd sit down at my kitchen table and write a letter of thanks to our client, asking them for feedback. In hindsight they were probably full of spelling mistakes because I can't write for toffee, but I would do it religiously. Then I'd visit them. Often back at the office we'd be high-fiving ourselves because we'd hit this month's numbers, but then we'd see the customer and they'd tell us the things that they were less happy about. It was hard to hear, but it helped us to close off gaps that might have given a competitor a chance to come in.

Understand your profit and loss account well

enough to know if something's not right

The only two businesses I've backed which have gone bust are those with founders who didn't understand their numbers. You have to be able to interpret your profit and loss figures, or find someone who can and value their input. I call it restaurant maths. Just like when you get a bill in a restaurant and think that something looks off, you should understand your accounts well enough to be able to say, 'Well, that doesn't look right. Or if it's right, we have a problem.' I've learned this lesson twice now, expensively.

PART 3

SELL

6

Putting Your House in Order

I f you've ever sold a house, this next phase of your business – the 'sell' period – will be familiar to you. First you have to make sure that it has great kerb appeal: is there any flaky paintwork on the front door, and could the garden look more inviting? Moving inside, is the decor well-presented and the living room nice and tidy? This is the equivalent of what a business buyer will be thinking when they look at your company: does it have a great brand, happy customers and an enviable reputation? And yet first impressions don't make up the whole story. Your buyer will also peel back the layers and inspect what's underneath. They'll go through your financial records, contracts, systems and anything else that could indicate the equivalent of rising damp or a subsidence problem, because there would be no point in them acquiring an asset that looks good on the surface but which is rotten underneath.

That's why this selling phase is the one in which

your main task is to make your business as attractive as possible, inside and out, to a potential buyer. For the next two or three years you're going to be in continual preparation mode for exit at the same time as running and growing your business just as you were before – it's a challenging combination.

As you read on you may feel daunted by how much there is to do, but it's worth bearing in mind that – while intense – the end is now in sight. As a long-distance cyclist, I know how much of a difference it makes when you're in the last few miles and the finish line is within touching distance. The sell period might take you less than three years or it might take you more, but whatever the duration, your job is to keep the end in mind all the way through. Your reward will come when you receive an offer that's way above what you would have achieved if you'd not prepared as well.

The basics

Before we go any further, it's helpful to understand the basic process for selling your business. It goes like this:

1. Make your business attractive to a buyer (takes three to four years).
2. Appoint an agent.
3. Gather the data for your memorandum of information, in conjunction with your agent and lawyers (takes five months minimum).
4. Put your business up for sale.
5. Attend pre-offer interviews with interested parties.
6. Receive offers.
7. Accept an offer (or offers) in principle.

8. Be interviewed by buyer(s) who've made an offer.
9. Provide extensive data to buyer(s), their accountants, agent and lawyers as part of their due diligence process. You'll also need to give them direct access to your customers.
10. Presentation(s) by your leadership team to buyer(s).
11. Accept a firm offer.
12. Sign off the sale.

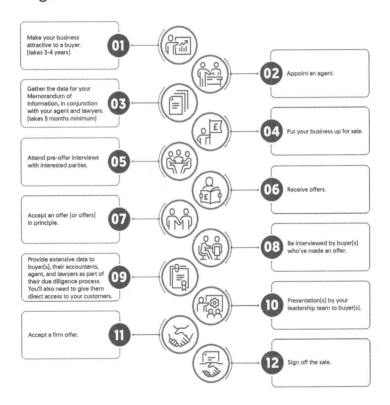

Make your business attractive to a buyer. (takes 3-4 years) **01**

02 Appoint an agent.

Gather the data for your Memorandum of Information, in conjunction with your agent and lawyers. (takes 5 months minimum) **03**

04 Put your business up for sale.

Attend pre-offer interviews with interested parties. **05**

06 Receive offers.

Accept an offer (or offers) in principle. **07**

08 Be interviewed by buyer(s) who've made an offer.

Provide extensive data to buyer(s), their accountants, agent, and lawyers as part of their due diligence process. You'll also need to give them direct access to your customers. **09**

10 Presentation(s) by your leadership team to buyer(s).

Accept a firm offer. **11**

12 Sign off the sale.

Of course, this is a standard process and yours may not go along these lines. You might not receive any offers; you may decide not to accept any of the ones that you're given; or you might 'fail' the due diligence process and have to start again. It's also worth bearing in mind that some of these steps run in parallel; for instance, you'll be continuing to make your business attractive to a buyer all the way through right up to the sale. We'll go through steps 1 to 3 in this chapter and the remainder in Chapter 8.

To start the process, what does a buyer look for when they're considering buying your company?

↗ a strategic fit between their business and yours
↗ a great brand and reputation
↗ financial records that show a history of progressive revenue growth, which continues right up to the sale itself
↗ plans that paint a picture of how future growth will be achieved
↗ a healthy profit margin with robust fiscal records
↗ watertight systems and processes that are working well and adhered to by all members of your business
↗ no legal 'black holes', in terms of staff and supplier contracts or data management compliance
↗ a senior leadership team which is capable of running the business without the founder.

Seen like that, it seems pretty reasonable. Your buyer wants to acquire a business that's likely to give them an excellent financial return and that at the same time presents as low a risk as possible. Imagine them holding a bucket full of money, and every time they have a concern about your company they take a wad of cash out of it. That's what will happen to your sale price if you disappoint them on any count. Which means that if you tick all the boxes to their satisfaction, you'll receive a higher price than if you don't.

Let's look at the main areas you need to focus on to keep that bucket as full as possible: strategic fit, brand reputation, compliance, growth and management.

Strategic fit

It sounds obvious, but a buyer will be looking to acquire a business that will help them to grow their own in some way. It might be for defensive reasons (to remove you as a threat if you're a competitor) or to expand their company by adding an extra element to it. In Smart Apprentices' case, our buyer had already produced a technology that did a similar job to our platform, but they were struggling to gain traction with it because ours was better and we had a stronger foothold in the market. That put us on their radar and meant we were a strategic fit for them. It didn't mean that they would automatically acquire us because there was another business that was up for sale at the same time which they could have bought instead. But for various reasons, they chose us.

Brand reputation

What your customers think about you is an important factor for your buyer. Bear in mind that you may share customers with them, so they will definitely talk to those customers to see what they think about you. Your acquirer will also be attracted by a strong brand and a refreshing marketing narrative.

Growth

Your scale-up phase was very much about growth rather than profit. However, in the selling phase your buyers will want to see that you're profitable and have been for a year or two at least. What's more, they need to be convinced that you're still growing your sales and profits right up to the purchase itself. And if that's not enough, you must also show that you have solid plans for how your company can continue to evolve in the future. Because the future is what your acquirer is buying, not the past. We'll talk more about revenue and profit growth in the next chapter.

Systems and compliance

After you've received an offer, your buyer will start the process of due diligence. In this, they crawl all over your financial, legal and strategic documentation. They'll use one of the top accounting firms to do this as well as their own lawyers, and they'll bring in sector experts to inspect your technology. There really is no place for you to hide in all this, so before you even think of putting your business up for sale you need to ensure that you're squeaky clean in every area. Using the house sale analogy again, you must have planning permission for all the renovations you've undertaken and be able to prove that the foundations and structure are strong.

Leadership

Now's the time to decide for sure whether you want to stay in your business after you sell or to exit along with the sale. I recommend the latter because from the conversations I've had with many entrepreneurs, staying on doesn't usually work well. For a start, your buyer will only pay you the full amount after you've hit certain KPIs – so you might receive 40 per cent at sale and then the rest as you achieve your targets (an earn-out). That can be difficult when you're no longer the CEO but a small cog in a big wheel. Who's to say you'll be able to get things done as quickly when you're not in control anymore? Not only will you lack the authority to demand what you once could, but you won't have the satisfaction of owning the business. Motivation can be low.

However, if you decide to exit along with the sale, there are things to take into account. Your buyer will want to see a leadership team that's fully functioning and able to run the business without you. And as part of making an offer, your acquirer will watch a presentation of your company's credentials by your top team, at which they'll grill them on every aspect of your business. This will be without your input. Would you be confident that your team could handle this seamlessly between them? If not, you have work to do.

When to sell

The decision about when to sell is a strategic one and mainly depends on the numbers you're hitting in your business. Your sale value is based on a multiple of your profits, so as soon as you've got to the right place you should start to get ready for sale. This doesn't always go according to plan. At Smart Apprentices we came close to the moment when we thought we were fit for sale, but then had a major setback with one of our new tech platforms. We spent the next few months going back to basics to fix it, which set us back considerably.

As well as figures, there's the question of your market. In an ideal world you'll be operating in a growing sector with few competitors, but as we all know that's rarely the case. So part of your decision should be based on whether now is the right time in terms of the environment you're operating in. If you predict that it will soon become less friendly than it is at the moment, it might be time to press the button.

Be prepared to move as soon as the time is right, because in a few months the situation might not be so rosy. What happens if your sales drop off? What if another pandemic hits? What if a new competitor appears out of the blue? What if your ideal buyer acquires another business that takes up all their resources? So much of getting the timing right is being ready to go, which is what this chapter will help you with.

Go it alone or use an agent?

I've sold two businesses, the first without an agent and the second with one. The first time I wasn't involved as I'd already left the company (I was only a shareholder by then, not an employee), and it was sold to a firm that was well known to the business. It's possible that we could have achieved a higher valuation if we'd used an agent but it was unlikely, as we'd aligned our technology so closely to our acquirer's that it restricted our exit options. However, at Smart Apprentices we used an agent, and it was definitely the right move for us. It gave us a wide reach and helped us to increase our value during the negotiation process because the agent managed that for us.

Where the agent was also invaluable was in the advice they gave us. When you sell a company you have to create a 'memorandum of information', which is essentially a sales pack that the agent sends to interested parties. Ours was 50 pages long, covering the company background, our numbers, business highlights, product development timelines, details about our shareholders, revenue models, legal compliance, all our operations, our people and organisational structure, our executive management team and future growth opportunities. It also showcased our products and outlined our markets, customers and competitors. Providing the information that went into creating the memorandum was a huge undertaking, and without our agent, Cavendish, we wouldn't have known where to start.

As well as the memorandum of information, Cavendish put together a two-page pitch document which they sent to anyone who expressed an initial interest. They also helped to prepare my leadership team for the due diligence process that would follow after offers were made, and for the presentation they'd have to give to the potential acquirer. Just as importantly, the agent ensured that they knew enough about Smart Apprentices to approach the right potential buyers – the ones who fitted my requirements. Because I was passionate about selling to a company that would protect our brand and people, not one that would strip out our assets and jettison the rest.

Preparations before you go up for sale

The purpose of the information-gathering above is

twofold: it provides the basis for the memorandum of information, and it forces you to go through the arduous task of finding and amending the materials that your eventual buyer will ask for. If they make you an offer it will be conditional on you passing their due diligence process, so if you don't do the information-gathering properly now you'll have a difficult time later on.

It's hard to get across the scale of the information that we had to provide, not only in terms of scope but also of depth. There must have been hundreds of different items, which we uploaded into a shared area. From there our lawyers were able to validate and risk assess them, and if anything was missing or incomplete we had to modify it. This meant that when we provided the information again for the buyer's due diligence (in completely different formats, of course – nothing is that simple), we were confident that it would hold water.

The whole process of sourcing and amending the data for the memorandum took five months of solid work. We gave the process a code name, Project End-to-End, so that everybody involved knew what it was about; also, it didn't raise suspicion for those who weren't included at that stage.

Here are the main things you'll be asked for (and be warned – you'll have to provide them in minute detail).

Legalities and processes

Although you're a relatively small company, your buyer will probably be a much larger one and they'll expect your contracts and processes to match their standards. That's because when they acquire you they also take on your liabilities, and the more of them they think there are, the lower the value of their offer will fall. For instance, there's a rule called IR35 which only applies to big companies. It means that when a business engages someone who's self-employed, PAYE and national insurance don't apply to any payments given to them. So the company's contracts must make it clear that the person isn't an employee, otherwise the business would be liable for their PAYE and national insurance along with a hefty fine from HMRC. When we'd drawn up our freelancer contracts, we hadn't thought to put in place any provision for this rule as it didn't apply to us at the time. But when we came to prepare for the sale, our lawyers told us that we had to redo the contracts otherwise our buyer would be exposed.

This is just one example of how lawyers will go through your employee, customer and supplier contracts with a fine-tooth comb and find all sorts of things wrong with them. Ours asked for 220 items, covering financials, technology, markets, assets, IP, HR, contracts, tax and capitalisation policy. They didn't hold back in telling us about anything they saw as problematic: 'We're not comfortable that you're protected against IR35 in that contract'; 'You have to go back to these suppliers and redo their contracts'; 'That agreement is out of date and doesn't feel robust enough'; 'What was the reason for the COT 3 redundancy?' It was never ending.

Inevitably we had to do a fair bit of retro-fitting, asking people to sign assignments of IP where they hadn't been done (or not in a way that stood up to the scrutiny of our lawyers). We hoped that people would be cooperative, which wasn't a problem if they were still working for us. But we also had to approach suppliers who we hadn't engaged with for some time, including one in India which had carried out some tech development for us. They did reassign the IP for us, probably in the hope that we'd give them more work in the future, but if they'd disappeared or not played ball it would have been a major problem.

That's why it's so much easier if you put your systems and legalities in place during the scale-up phase, rather than when you come to sell. The main red flag areas for us were employment contracts and assignments of IP, but for you they may be different. Even though our company was in better shape than many I've come across, there was a lot of cleaning up to do.

Financials

When your buyer does their due diligence they'll ask their accountants to crawl over your financial and tax records for the previous two years, the current year, and your projections for the next three years. They could go back further if they feel there's a need to, for instance if they're concerned about your business not growing for a while three or four years back. They'll want to know why.

With financial records there's not the same opportunity to retrofit them as there is with other contracts as once they they have been submitted they cannot be altered. It's pointless to try and bluff your way through any issues because you'll be found out pretty quickly; you're just wasting everyone's time. If you have worries about how some of your figures will look, your time is better spent working out a credible explanation of why that is and what you've done to put the situation right.

When you eventually sell you'll also need to provide warranties to your buyer, which state that you're compliant on your tax, that you haven't made any VAT or tax errors for the past few years and that all your computations are accurate and honest. If your acquirer has an HMRC inspection after they've bought you and finds that you didn't comply with your tax obligations three years ago, they'll come after you personally for that money. The good news is that if you've run a good, clean business from the start you shouldn't have any problems with giving warranties.

Products, markets and customers

We had to profile all our different products and state what percentage we'd sold to which customers during the past two years as well as validate our projections for the next three years. We also had to say what products we intended to sell to which customers to achieve our growth over the next three years and prove that we had good reasons for claiming that. Your buyer will lift the lid on your assertions and look at how many products you've sold, at what price, who to, whether you discounted them and how your figures compare to those of your competitors. If you've artificially increased your sales by lowering your prices, it will soon show.

The area of sales projections is another one in which it would be tempting to tell a good story in the hope that it will stick, but you won't get away with this if you can't back it up. We created three years' worth of projections, with our buyer looking mainly at the current year, the previous two years and three years into the future. Given that it's a five- or six-year window of financial data that you're presenting, you have to make sure that your strategy is robust and that your numbers stack up.

Senior leadership team

In the presentation that your team will eventually give to a potential buyer, they'll be closely questioned. Suppose that your memorandum of information states that 97 per cent of your customers renew each year. Your buyer might want to know what you do about the customers you lose. What are your customer satisfaction scores? How often do you survey your customer base? Where's the data about it? And how do you measure the satisfaction of different stakeholders? Your leadership team should have all this information to hand, and they must be aligned on every issue. Because every time they answer a question evasively or disagree with one another, it's like taking a wad of cash out of that bucket. (Alternatively, you may be required to stay on and run the business for two or three years).

This means that you need to involve your team with the gathering of information for the memorandum. They need to be able to answer any questions about it just as well as you can, and in a way that shows they're in alignment with one another. Through this, you're carrying on the process of disentangling yourself from your business which you began in the scale-up phase, with the aim of enabling your top team to present a united front at the end.

Preparing your senior leadership team

This area is so important that it's worth further exploration. I remember having to sit in the room while my senior team presented my business (yes, it still felt like 'my business') to our potential buyers and not being able to say a word. I watched them being grilled by the buying team and also knew that they would be interviewed individually about my involvement in the business and to see if they were fit to run it after I'd gone. I could never have put them up for this if I hadn't spent the two or three years in the run-up to the sale ensuring that they were ready for the task. I didn't bring anyone new into the team during that time, and I made sure that my sales director could sell better than me, that my operations director could explain our systems and processes better than me, that my technology director understood our platform better than me and that they were led by a strong leader in the form of Ann, our MD (not me!).

It was even more important for me to feel confident in them because I wanted a buyer who would keep them on, not one who would use the technology assets from Smart Apprentices and nothing else. I very much wanted to find a home for my product and people to do well in, and for that reason sought an acquirer whose values and ethics fitted with mine. It was what everyone deserved.

The roles

It's essential to have top-quality people in your senior team, and for them to be in the right roles. My sales director was responsible for new business and my customer services director for renewals; I made sure that they had the motivation to work well together. They each received commission based on the revenue they generated and they worked together to onboard new customers so that there was a smooth handover. Everything went into our CRM system and everything was KPI'd – it was a transparent process.

My managing director was obviously a pivotal member of the senior team. I brought her in towards the end of the scale-up phase, so she'd been in post for three years by the time we exited. She'd originally been our head of user experience, but I saw that she had MD potential and it made sense to promote internally because she already had a good relationship with the leadership team. At first I was like a shadow MD, mentoring her to take over the role, but after a while I realised that this wasn't empowering her as much as it could. It took me a year to have the confidence that I'd put the right person in place and to let go of the strategic reins, which meant that I could spend more of my time preparing for the exit. I also remunerated her based on new and existing revenue, rather than product development and enhancement, as I knew that this was what a buyer would be most interested in. She thrived when I stepped back.

Working together

Your buyer may take your directors out to dinner to get

to know them, so if there's any bad blood between the team members it will soon become apparent. You need them to work harmoniously together, not just to deliver the numbers but also to avoid raising a red flag for the buyer. If there's even one person who isn't performing well, they'll spot it.

That means you have to try your best to anticipate some of the questions that will come their way. Your people may be asked the same question but at different times, or to different members of the team, so they need to be aligned in their views. If they're asked about a particular point in your product strategy document from three years ago, would they all give a similar response?

Your leadership team and you

One of the things that I found hardest during the run-up to the exit was relinquishing the day-to-day control of my senior team. It was important that our buyer shouldn't see my fingerprints over everything, so I had to let go of the reins. This at least gave me the benefit of some extra time to prepare for other aspects of the sale.

I was already aware of what would be involved because I'd been on a training course about selling a company. I knew what kind of information we'd need to provide and how the business would be valued. But I still had to meet agents who could represent the business and equip myself to steer us through the sale process.

Although pulling together the information for the memorandum of information was an enormous task, I had a business to run at the same time. I couldn't ask my leadership team to stop what they were doing to help, because their responsibility was to hit the right numbers so that we could achieve a great sale price. I was working 20 hours a day, six days a week, for five months solid, and I could only talk to a limited number of people about what was going on.

You may be wondering when is the best time to share your intention with your key people. It depends on who they are and what they already know. Two of my team had been with me from the start and were aware of my eventual plan, but I didn't tell the others until I'd started the process with the agent. It was important to me that they knew I wanted to find a quality buyer who would look after them and that they would be a key part in us achieving that.

It helped that I'd already incentivised them with shares, which meant that they could receive some of the sale proceeds at exit. In fact, our buyer also put an incentive on the table for all my leadership team to stay on. If your acquirer doesn't offer something similar and you want to encourage your team to continue in the new business (so that you're not required to stay on yourself), you could include a loyalty bonus in their employment contracts. Their new employer doesn't have to keep it, but it's normal for them to honour existing terms.

We appointed an agent in September and by the following February we'd provided all the vetted and amended data. That was when they completed the memorandum of information, and we went up for sale in March. From February to March, we worked hard to prepare the presentation that my leadership team would have to give to any buyers who made an offer.

This was a pitch that only they could make, so it was essential that they had a full understanding of what they were going to say and were all on the same page. Oh, and just to complicate things, this was all during the Covid-19 pandemic.

Quick recap

- ↗ To achieve the best possible value for your business, it needs to have both external and internal appeal.
- ↗ Your business must keep growing profitably right up to the time of sale.
- ↗ There's a huge amount of work involved in providing the data required for the memorandum of information.
- ↗ You need to justify every figure, projection and assertion about your business.
- ↗ If you want to exit along with your business, your senior leadership team should be running the company effectively well before the time that you sell.

Questions to ask yourself

- ↗ Put yourself in a buyer's shoes. What strengths and weaknesses would your business have from their point of view?
- ↗ What can you do to strengthen the areas that are problematic?
- ↗ Who in your leadership team will you tell about the sale, and when?
- ↗ What do you need to learn about the selling process and how can you do it?
- ↗ How are you going to find the time to go through this process?

An Entrepreneur's Experience

Varun Gupta

Varun is currently founder of Torchlight Advisors, an India-centric investment and advisory firm focusing on tech start-ups and distressed investments. Prior to that he was co-founder of Lifafa, a board observer at SmartE and Hotelogix, and CEO of GOOMO. He set up GOOMO in 2016 as an omni-channel travel distribution platform, selling not only to consumers but to travel agents as well. The business went from zero to $250 million turnover in four years, employing more than 500 people across 15 locations. In March 2020, when Covid-19 struck, it hit rock bottom.

I asked Varun to share with me the lessons he's learned about starting and scaling a business. Here are some of the highlights.

Sometimes things go badly wrong and it's not your fault, but how you respond is

When Covid-19 hit the travel industry, our investors sent me a presentation by McKinsey saying that the pandemic would last for two and a half years. I didn't believe it; like everyone else at that time, I thought it would be a few weeks. But I wasn't able to convince our investors of this, who walked out because they thought the risk was too high. Three major airline suppliers declared bankruptcy, then one of our biggest customers also went bust.

So I sat down and considered my options. The best piece of advice I received was 'For everyone else it's money, but for you it's personal.' I could have abandoned my business and gone back to the safe world of corporate accounting, but knew I had to ride out the crisis and save my reputation. I decided to leave India for the UK so that I could gain a fresh perspective, and started the process of closing the business down. However, when I was down to 11 people, I managed to win a few fights and received a bit of money from some old creditors. That was the beginning of my journey back up.

Use the money you have, not the money you'd like to have

The typical entrepreneurial approach is to raise funds so that you can create the product you want. After Covid-19, when our funds dried up, my only option was to change the approach: 'This is the money I have, so let's figure out what I can do with it.' As an entrepreneur, everything you're able to do is a function of money. It forces you to make tough choices about people, facilities, the product and customer service. Because of the pandemic, GOOMO stopped being a 24/7 business, which might seem like sacrilege in travel, but the cost wasn't worth it. I lost a lot of customers as a result, but it was the choice I made to keep the business afloat.

Running out of cash is the best entrepreneurial MBA in the world

There's no book that can teach you everything you need to know about entrepreneurship. You have to go through the bad times – that's the only way you really learn. It's those bad times that teach you whether or not you're cut out for it. I'm not afraid of a fight anymore.

Look after yourself when times are hard

The first time I was splashed across the front page of a

newspaper for firing people, I couldn't get out of bed for three days. What kept me going through the nightmare of my business coming close to collapse was exercising every day and finding distractions. I like cooking, so I cooked with my family throughout the pandemic. And I started to meditate, which calmed me down. I also talked to people about my fear of being judged, and this made me a lot more open; I'm not the strong, silent type anymore. It's okay to be scared, and it's okay to say that you're scared.

The exit shouldn't be your focus

There are some golden rules with entrepreneurship. One is that you need a business where the unit economics are strong. Another is that you need to be able to scale the business. The third is that you must have the right team. And the fourth is that you shouldn't focus on the exit; your strategy should be to make the business profitable. If it is, a successful exit will follow.

It takes a certain kind of person to be an entrepreneur

Only two types of people become entrepreneurs: extremely stupid and extremely optimistic ones. Also, extremely stubborn. I'm probably all three.

7

Maintaining Your Growth

As any entrepreneur knows, what matters most in a business is the numbers. And so it will be for your eventual acquirer – they'll look first and foremost at your sales and profits when they decide whether or not to make you an offer. Of course, all the other aspects of your business need to line up for them as well, but it's the financials that will be at the forefront of their decision making. That's why your sales and profits need to keep growing right until the point of sale, a process which can take three or four years before you reach the right place. In fact, increasing your revenue and profits is where you need to start the selling phase – it's the bedrock of achieving a high valuation.

But there's more. Whoever acquires you won't want to buy a product that's at the end of its life cycle. They'll want something that's still flourishing, with lots of potential – like a house that's in an up-and-coming neighbourhood. They're buying the future, not the past, so you have to show that the future of your business is rosy. That means creating a strategy for growth that will take your business well into the next few years, even if you want to sell it before then. There's a lot to think about, so in this chapter we'll look at what it means to grow your sales, how you can increase your profits and what a future strategy could look like.

Growing your revenue

In Chapter 5 I talked about how important it is to keep ramping up your sales in the scale-up phase and how one way of doing that is to look at 'share of wallet'. With this, you identify complementary products that you can develop to sell to your existing customers. This can also help you to retain those customers, because they have another reason to stay with you.

During the scale-up phase at Smart Apprentices, we developed five new products. One of them was created for an adjacent market so that we could extend our footprint and was a direct response to the government's changes to legislation for apprenticeships. We realised that there was an opportunity we could take advantage of, and that there was nothing on the market that already existed to cater for it. In terms of sales, it was our most successful new product development outside our main platform.

The other four products were for existing customers. One was the English and maths assessment tool that I described in Chapter 5, which was inspired by a technology that one of our largest competitors had developed (although we made sure that ours was better). It was hard at first to tempt colleges away from the competitor product, but once we got some early adopters using and talking about it, it gained traction. Selling this helped us in two ways: it gave us more revenue and, because it was integrated into our existing product, it provided another tentacle for us to hook into our customers. Once a customer was using it in conjunction with our existing platform, it meant that they'd be less likely to switch to a competitor product because they'd have to transfer two products rather than one.

Next came two further products, which were also upsells to existing customers. One was called Smart Annotation, which gave assessors the ability to watch a video made by their students and to comment directly on the recording. There was nothing like this on the market and they loved it. The other was Smart Data, which was a Microsoft Power BI dashboard that pulled data from all our platforms to create one single data view. Colleges loved this too. Both products were relatively inexpensive to create (the dashboard cost us less than £10,000, compared to our average spend of hundreds of thousands on a new product) and we used external developers so that we didn't have to increase our headcount. What's more, it illustrated that we were always far more innovative than our competitors and this helped us to retain existing clients and gain an additional share of their wallets.

The fifth and final product, which was also for our existing customers, was called Smart Applicants. It created a revenue opportunity for colleges by allowing them to expand their footprint into new services such as supporting people back into work. Because it was the last new product we developed, we only started selling it just before we exited, but it meant that we could put it into our future revenue plan. We already had a track record of developing products, taking them to market and selling them to existing customers, so it was a credible way of giving our buyer confidence that the business would continue to grow in the years to come.

This is why it's so important to keep developing and improving your products through both the scale-up and selling phase – you'll reap the rewards when it comes to the sale. What's more, you don't know yet when your exit will happen; you can't even be sure that you'll be successful the first time around. So you need to keep growing and making yourself a desirable brand, with the aim of attracting interest from the right buyer at the right price when the time comes.

Most challenging of all, you can't be seen to be doing all this yourself as a founder. If you're talented at selling you have to let your sales director take the lead, and if you're a tech founder your IT director must be the one to take charge of new product development. Try to see this as an opportunity to spend time on preparing for exit – this is now your main focus as far as products and sales are concerned.

Growing your profits

So far we've talked about revenue growth but not so much about growth of profits. When you were scaling-up, your profit levels weren't your main concern – you had to invest in order to grow and it was acceptable for your margins to take a hit. But now that you're coming up to the sale of your business, you need to make sure that you increase your profits at the same time as continuing to grow your revenues.

That's because your sale value will most likely be

based on a multiple of your profit. Exactly what the multiple is depends on the kind of business you have. If it's a tech business it's usually between eight and 12 times your EBIT (earnings before interest and tax); if it's a non-tech business it will be less. It's possible that your company will be valued based on your annual renewable revenue rather than your profit level, but this is less common. So profits are key if you're to sell for as high a value as possible.

This can involve creating a culture shift in your company – moving from increasing sales at all costs to doing it in a way that avoids spending too much money in the process. Here are some ways to increase your profit levels in the years running up to exit.

Reduce product development

Hopefully you've done enough product development in your scale-up phase to be able to reduce your technology investment now but at the same time reap the rewards of what you've created. That's the main way that we achieved our profit growth during the exit phase; if we hadn't been prepared with new products, we wouldn't have been half as successful at creating a high value when it came to the sale. On one product alone we made nearly 20 per cent of our total revenue by selling it to three new customers. That gave our acquirer a lot of confidence that we were able to develop new platforms and sell them successfully.

Having said that, it's important not to drop all product development completely. Not only will this put you in a poor position in terms of your future growth strategy, but it will also be apparent to a buyer as soon as they lift the lid on your accounts that you've suddenly become more profitable because you're not investing in your future. So cherry pick which product developments you plan to invest in and make sure they're based on innovative ideas that nobody else has thought of. This will future-proof your business with an ongoing competitive advantage.

Ramp up your sales effort

In the selling phase you're wanting to prove to a buyer that the investments you've made in product development during the scale-up period are coming to fruition. That means doing all you can to sell new products to existing customers and your existing products to new customers. Because if your forward trajectory is based on the sunk cost of the investment you've already made, your new sales will be pure profit in the future.

Retain your existing customers

Your buyer doesn't want to acquire a leaky bucket that's losing customers, even while gaining new ones. If you're finding that your churn levels are high, ask yourself why you're losing customers. Where are they going? What's in it for them to shift to a new supplier? It's so much more expensive and difficult to win new business than it is to keep existing revenue that this really is worth your time and attention.

Review your pricing

Like many businesses, we originally attracted some of our first customers at relatively low prices and had close relationships with them which we nurtured over the years. They'd helped us to grow our brand and had introduced us to new customers, so we owed them a lot. But the time came when we had to increase what we charged them so as to align them more closely with other customers. Naturally we couldn't simply double what we charged – that would have been far too risky. But we could upsell our new products to them at a premium price to make up part of the difference.

We also spent a lot of time unravelling our various customer profiles, reviewing how much we charged them in relation to the usage they were getting out of our platform. This involved us becoming more rigorous about counting the licences that we'd issued, and was a change from our scale-up phase when we were more concerned about driving new sales.

Staffing levels

Because of our slowdown in new product development, we were able to reduce our headcount proportionately by not bringing any new people into the business. This also saved us the money that we would have spent on recruitment consultants and onboarding recruits.

Growing your future

When a buyer first casts their eye over your business, they're naturally interested in what's going on right now. But far more important to them is what they consider to be its future potential. After all, they can't make any money on what you've sold in the past, but they do intend to make money on what they could sell in the years to come. This means that you need a strategy in place that paints a robust picture of your company's future. Your buyer wants to feel excited about the opportunities that will open up as a result of acquiring your business, not wondering what they'll do with it once it's theirs.

Your future strategy

That was why we created an exciting future for Smart Apprentices. It was a brand-new learning experience platform that we presented as something we would build, but at the point at which we went up for sale it was in the prototyping phase only. The impetus for it came because of what was happening in our marketplace. New entrants were entering with more integrated solutions than ours, and while they weren't really hurting us yet as their technology was lightweight, I could see the potential for them to become serious contenders. It was obvious that we needed to stay several steps ahead of them, so two years before we exited I took the strategic decision to start designing and developing the new platform. Its purpose was to help learners develop their skills and knowledge in a new, adaptive platform that none of our competitors had thought of; it would be highly innovative and also, by using artificial intelligence, be future proof.

To create the strategy, I spent a lot of time exploring and experimenting with what I thought the future of learning in our sector would look like. This involved meeting with a professor of artificial intelligence who specialised in learning and investing time researching publications by KPMG, Goldman Sachs and Harvard Business School. I learned that, despite unemployment being high, there were a lot of job vacancies that weren't being filled. Why was that? It was clear to me that re-skilling would be a massive part of the future, especially post Brexit. I could also see that automation was going to eliminate some jobs and that much learning now is informal; we find out new things by going online or asking a friend.

The new learning platforms that I could see already in the market weren't fully recognising these trends or that learning is lifelong and that there will always be a need for people to improve their skills. That's why we didn't copy any of our competitors – it would be pointless to mimic or even improve on what they were doing. I went back to basics and asked myself: 'What does the future of learning look like? How can we create a platform that provides our users with an end-to-end solution that's the only one they'll need for years to come?'

Because my plan was so futuristic I knew I couldn't just ask our customers if they wanted it, because some of it was beyond their current understanding. And yet it was also important that they came with us on the journey; only they could decide how the new platform might (or might not) work for them. So I had to balance the need to be visionary with the need to create something that we could sell. We spent a whole year carrying out customer workshops and focus groups to see if my ideas would land with our customers. Would any be rejected out of hand? Were there some that could be made real?

By the time we came to sell the business we'd started building the platform and were on the way to creating our first minimum viable product (MVP). We had investment in place, but we made sure that all our supplier contracts had exit clauses every three months. This cost us more, but we did it so that if an acquirer decided they didn't want to continue with the development after buying us, there was a 'get out of jail free' card for them.

Hopefully you can see the value of having a future development prototyped, designed, costed and with supplier agreements in place, so that all it would take for your buyer to benefit from it is to press 'go'. It's a virtual extension of your business, just as you might gain planning permission for an extension to your house if you were going to sell it. You're saying to a buyer, 'Look, you can build this. Here are the plans, here's the permission and here are the costs from the builder – all you have to do is give the go-ahead if you want it.'

It's a balancing act

When you create a strategy for the future you're walking a tightrope because you don't know who you're going to sell to. Your buyer might already have created something similar to what's in your plan and therefore not be interested in it, but if that's the case they don't have to build it. You want to give them as many options as possible, while at the same time pointing towards a bright destiny that's optional for them. In some ways this is similar to the balancing act you're treading all the way to exit, delivering on the now but also creating an exciting prospect for your acquirer to buy into for the future.

Quick recap

- ↗ During the exit phase it's just as important to keep increasing your sales as it is at any other time in your business, right up to the point of sale.
- ↗ You also need to focus on increasing your profits, possibly for the first time.
- ↗ A strategic plan which creates a positive vision of the future will help to attract a buyer.

Questions to ask yourself

- ↗ How can I keep increasing my revenue right up until the end?
- ↗ Where am I losing profits and where am I making them?
- ↗ How can I make more profit?
- ↗ What's the future for our sector?
- ↗ Can I create a future plan that makes the most of the opportunities available to us?

An Entrepreneur's Experience

Ian Cassidy

Ian specialises in growing brands. He's helped hundreds of the world's top brands to become more relevant to their consumers, while also driving two of his own companies towards successful exits.

He turned TBG Digital into an 'Agency of the Year', leading to an exit to Sprinklr in 2015. That same year he founded SHARE Creative, which was acquired by Samy in 2020. Today Ian is an advisor at Sether, the world's first blockchain-powered marketing platform, helping it to scale after a successful ICO (initial coin offering). Currently his focus is on driving growth within the Samy Group, both from organic client acquisition and driving forward their merger and acquisition activities.

I asked Ian to share with me the lessons he's learned about starting, scaling and selling a business. Here are some of the highlights.

The best way to find friends and supporters is to help people. Make superstars of your employees

I was an army child, changing schools every year, so I had to find friends quickly wherever I went. I found that the best way of doing that was to help people. When it came to the point at which I wanted to build a marketing agency, I knew that it had to have the purpose of making superstars of its staff. A lot of London agencies at the time were those clichéd ones with a big boss at the top telling people what to do, going to massive lunches and bossing a PA around.

It used to make me cringe. I thought there was a better way. Today, I get my energy from the people around me being super excited that they've achieved their dreams or received recognition for what they've done.

Having a strong company purpose attracts the right people

Our purpose at SHARE is to be an agency of reference – the one that's talked about in universities as the place that sets the standard for something. Being a reference point gives people a lot of motivation to join and become aligned to that purpose.

When things go badly only you, the founder, can make the difficult decisions

For a while we grew incredibly quickly and thought we were unassailable, but then we lost three of our biggest clients in a row. This caused a cash flow crisis and we had to say goodbye to some really amazing people, which was hard. That was when I learned that I really was the founder and the only person prepared to make the toughest decisions.

Timing can be cruel

One day after the difficult conversations I had to have with my staff during the redundancies, I was at home moping about and wondering how we were going to get ourselves out of the situation. A potential client who we'd done a huge pitch to called and said, 'I've got some great news for you.' They became (and remain) our largest client to this day. I fell back on the sofa and the first person I called was one of the key members of my management team, who'd been a casualty of the job losses. 'Mate, you don't need to go freelance now,' I said. He was delighted, but sadly we lost two or three brilliant talents who we couldn't bring back. In fact, that was probably one of the factors that drove me to sell the business; having the backing of a bigger company would mean less pressure on cash flow and that we could hire in advance.

Handing the sale yourself is possible

Apart from some external help with the finance, I handled the sale of my company by myself. One of the first potential acquirers I spoke to asked for a mergers and acquisitions (M&A) pack, so I googled 'M&A pack' and bought one. Completing it was made easier by the fact that I knew everything about our accounts: every invoice and every deferred revenue. The buyer said that it was the best finance pack he'd ever seen in his life. Also, I knew the acquirers I was talking to. For each, I tailored our purpose and values to how they would align with theirs and what we could offer them if we were to integrate. A third-party agency would never have known all that, and they'd have taken a percentage cut as well.

Doing an earn-out can work
if both parties are aligned

When I was eventually acquired by Samy, its offer was for me to carry on running SHARE Creative and to build the brand, expand into the US and create other agencies. I wanted to do the earn-out as it was my aim to be as helpful as I could. It was also satisfying to defy expectations because people don't expect you to stay to the end. But to me, if you don't want to stay with your acquirer, why sell to them? Samy has been a great buyer because it's given me the autonomy to continue being an entrepreneur.

You need another challenge after the exit

My next challenge is to take SHARE Creative to an IPO because if I don't have something to strive for I feel depressed and lost. Having the backing of my acquirer has made a huge difference to how ambitious I can be; we're now at 100 per cent growth year on year and I have big plans for the future.

8

The Sale

After all the work we'd done on growing our business and pulling together the memorandum of information, it should have been a relief when we were finally ready to put our business up for sale, but it was actually pretty nerve wracking. We went through all our data one last time with our lawyers and agent, then the moment came when everyone was happy and we were good to go. But would any bidders put an offer in, and if they did, for what amounts?

In the end we received three serious offers, which was amazing because businesses going up for sale don't always receive any the first time round. Two were from companies that I didn't feel were a good fit, but one was from a larger player in our sector which I considered to be the business I'd have chosen from the beginning if I could. To crown it off, they also put in the best offer. There was one catch – they demanded exclusivity, which meant that we had to turn down the other two offers before we went through the due diligence process. However, our agent mitigated this by insisting on a four-week limit on the exclusivity. If our bidder didn't complete their due diligence in four weeks, we could go back on the market.

Pre-offer meetings

Before the offers you receive are firmed up, you'll be asked to attend pre-offer interviews. These are conversations between you, as founder, and your bidders, to see if it's a suitable match on both sides. Mine took around two hours each and were pretty gruelling. It had been a long time since I'd been interviewed by anyone, and there was a panel of them on one side of the table and me on the other. However, it was a two-way street because I wanted to make sure that they were a good match for my business and the people who were staying on in it. I also had to be careful because the bidders wanted to find out about my entrepreneurial journey and my aspirations for Smart Apprentices' future. I didn't want to stay on in the business, so I had to make sure that they knew it wasn't Fiona Hudson-Kelly they were buying but my business, and that my senior team had been taking the lead in growing the business for some time.

It was through these interviews that I discovered two of our bidders weren't a good fit for us. One was an IT company in our sector that didn't 'get' our culture; it seemed like they were going to exploit my people and brand rather than nurture the business. Another was a training company rather than a technology company, and I wanted Smart Apprentices to be part of a larger tech business that could use its expertise to accelerate our development. However, the final one was the ideal bidder for me because it operated in a similar way to us, and I could see that it was committed to taking on my people and developing our platform in a way that aligned with my values.

After the pre-offer meetings, I discussed the bids with my agent. Even prior to the interviews I knew a fair bit about the bidders, as they operated in our space. If I hadn't, I'd have carried out more research and asked our customers what they were like to deal with. Also, the agent was helpful in terms of strategic advice and they knew what kind of buyer I wanted.

Although it was my decision who to proceed with, I did discuss it with my senior team. It was important to me that they were happy with the choice. Luckily it was an easy one because we all agreed on who we should go with – it was a dream match. And while accepting the exclusive offer was a bit scary because it meant blowing the other two bidders out of the water, I went for it. An exciting and nerve-wracking process was about to begin.

The road to completion

Just like when you sell a house, your buyer's offer isn't firm until they've completed a survey. In the case of selling a business, this survey is made up of two parts: a management presentation to the potential acquirer and the buyer's own due diligence process.

The presentation to the buyer

This is your acquirer's first opportunity to meet your leadership team and they'll use it to suss out whether or not your company is well led and managed. In my case it was even more important as it had to prove to our buyer that it could run without me.

Selling a business during one of the Covid-19 lockdowns was a strange experience. People had just been given permission to meet face to face for urgent business meetings, so my leadership team and I travelled down to London for the pitch. The city was a ghost town. There was nobody on the train, nobody on the streets, nobody in the car park and nobody at the hotel where we did the presentation. The whole thing felt surreal.

As we walked into the room we were faced with a range of people, lined up both virtually and in person. There was the group CEO, the divisional MD and other senior members of their leadership team. I could see that the people I'd met at the pre-offer interview were no longer directly involved; we'd moved up a level now. On the other side of the room was my leadership team, with me sitting to one side as they had to do the presentation on their own. The presentation and questions lasted for about four hours and everything went really well. We could tell that there was a positive culture fit and a great synergy between us. As well as us pitching to them, their group CEO also presented their vision, values, culture and direction of future travel. They talked about why they wanted to buy us and how Smart Apprentices would fit into their company. This was important for my leadership team to see, so that they could feel confident they'd have a home in the new business. After the presentation our buyer made a firm offer, but the work wasn't over yet.

The completion

Our sale was the fastest our agent had ever experienced; we went up for sale in mid-March, did the pre-offer interviews and received the exclusive offer on 5 April. Later in April we did the presentation to our chosen buyer and the whole transaction was completed by 17 May. The process was expedited by the four-week window our buyer had to work within, but what also helped was that we'd done so much preparation beforehand in order to create our memorandum of information. This meant that, when the buyer came to do their due diligence, we were able to give them all the information their lawyers and accountants asked for quickly. Even though they asked many additional questions to the ones we'd already answered in the memorandum, we could provide most of the answers by slicing and dicing the existing data in different ways.

And yet it was still nerve wracking because the deal could be scuppered at any time. Once our buyer was able to lift the lid on our business and have a rummage around, there was no telling if they'd find something they didn't like. Luckily there were no show-stoppers, so we launched into a chaotic flurry of paperwork to complete the sale process. We were supposed to sign on a Friday and complete the same day, but the money didn't arrive because it was delayed in the US, so we had to wait until the Monday. And then it was done! We couldn't go out to celebrate because restaurants were still locked down, so given we were allowed small groups at home, some of the senior team came over to my house for a Chinese takeaway and a well-deserved glass of champagne. I wanted to capture the moment as it happened.

My next task was to announce the sale to everyone in my business (I still thought of it as 'my' business – that would have to change). Until then, nobody apart from my top team knew that we were going to sell. I wanted people to know it was something I'd chosen, that we weren't in any trouble and that it was a positive step for the company. Given that we couldn't meet in person I announced it on Zoom, which didn't feel too strange as we were already used to working remotely. However, it was surreal for me personally because I knew that I'd never see some of these people again. I received some lovely messages afterwards, which was bittersweet. After that there was a week of supporting the buyer to enable them to meet everyone, and then suddenly there was nothing for me to do. It was over.

How does it feel?

There are no words to describe what it's like to sell your business. During the preparations for it I sometimes felt a little remorseful and sad, and even wondered if I was doing the right thing. It felt strange to see my buyer talking with my leadership team (or rather, *their* leadership team), especially when they started discussing plans for the future, which I wouldn't be part of. And then to have nothing to do – no diary commitments, no to-do list – felt alien. I'd always been busy, so not being needed anymore was bizarre.

The money

All the work you do to sell your business is in aid of one thing: receiving a cash payment. Well, maybe it's not the only thing – you want your company to have a good home as well. But as with everything in business, the numbers are key.

So how did I feel when the money landed in my bank account? My share of the company was 95 per cent, which amounted to tens of millions of pounds. That level of wealth is unimaginable for most people, and was to me too. Not many people have achieved that, and it put me in the top 3 per cent of business owners who've sold their companies. You might imagine that I'd be jumping for joy and throwing wads of cash around like confetti, but it wasn't like that at all. I felt just as responsible for the money as I had for my business, and it was really stressful. Even the thought of it sitting in my bank account was a concern. I wanted it to make a difference, not only to me and my family, but also to others who hadn't had the opportunities that I'd been able to give to my children.

So although the money wasn't unexpected, I found myself not wanting to keep it. As a child I'd grown up with nothing and had to earn every penny for myself, an experience which has given me a frugal approach to life. For instance, I've just booked a flight to Australia to see two of my children, and I couldn't bring myself to pay for business class. It just felt wrong. I've never had expensive tastes and think of myself as a pretty ordinary person, so I wanted to stay grounded in the way I spent the proceeds of the sale. Buying yachts and designer handbags is really not 'me'.

I'd assumed that there would be somebody to guide me through the process of deciding what to do with the money, but there was no one person I could trust. Due to the large sum my account got moved to Coutts Bank, which triggered requests from a flurry of advisors who were all keen to help me decide how to spend it. In the end I found several experts to work with but even they were reluctant to give me concrete advice. They presented me with options but I had to figure out my own way forward. It was a steep learning curve.

Part of the difficulty was learning about tax regulations, which dictated what I could and couldn't do. I was about to turn 60, so inheritance tax was something that I had my eye on; I'd already paid 20 per cent capital gains tax on the sale proceeds and didn't want my kids to have to give another 40 per cent away. I also wanted to reward the people who'd helped me to build my business, which meant that I had to navigate rules about gifting.

What felt more positive, though, was to invest in my new businesses and my philanthropy. I've started a platform to help entrepreneurs, and I'll use it to give bursaries and support to new start-ups. It's important to me to do something meaningful with my money.

After the exit

In the Scale part of this book, I talked briefly about planning for what you'll do after the exit. This is so important. It can be difficult to do because I know from experience that it feels as if you may jinx the sale, but if you don't have some idea about how you're going to spend your time after you've sold your business you'll find that your whole world comes to a juddering halt. It's like walking off the edge of a cliff. Everything you've known – your work, your relationships with your colleagues – is suddenly gone.

Most entrepreneurs don't retire. Many go on to invest in other businesses and this gives them a reason to get fired up in the morning, meet people and have a purpose in life. We humans like to strive; you can see that in how we save up for things before we buy them. It's more satisfying that way. If money is no longer an object and you can buy pretty much whatever you want, how will you make life meaningful for yourself? I'd assumed that I'd do a big trek in Nepal or Australia and spend a few months re-calibrating, but Covid-19 put paid to that. So I had to ask myself how I wanted to spend the next phase of my life and come up with some answers.

I had always imagined when I sold Smart Apprentices that I would use my wealth to invest in other people's companies as an angel investor, which is often what successful entrepreneurs do after they sell.

However, I quickly realised that this wasn't for me. I was horrified at how many early start-up founders inflated the value of their business, asking for a crazy amount of money for very little equity, and it baffled me how quickly they were burning through other people's money without caring about growing revenue or a clear route to profit.

I did a lot of soul searching and decided that I had always been most successful when I backed myself.

So, with hardly a breath, I've recruited a fabulous

small team, including the key leadership roles of finance, technology and marketing. Together we're having fun creating a number of new technology platforms based on ideas I've had and bringing them to market. I've still got the motivation to replicate, and maybe better, the successful exit I had with Smart Apprentices.

It's different not having to worry about money during the start-up phase; while it's easier, I'm not sure its better – being too comfortable can mean you get distracted with perfecting products instead of getting them to market quickly and developing them with real customers.

I'm keeping this book next to me to remind myself to focus on acquiring and retaining customers and the rest will follow.

Start Scale Sell

Start Scale Sell is the new business that's most important to me. It's a tech platform which is structured around the same three phases as this book: starting a business, scaling it and selling it. Within each phase, entrepreneurs can assess themselves to work out where they are on their business journey and what they need to learn. They can then access help in two ways: by asking questions of other entrepreneurs who are strong in the areas they're weak in and by connecting with resources and advisors. Through this, they can fill their knowledge gaps.

I can't help everyone one to one, so this platform is a chance for me to share my expertise and that of other people who've successfully sold their companies. I'm passionate about helping business owners who are struggling to grow because I didn't have this kind of support when I first started out. I want more people to think of entrepreneurship as an option for them, and to see what founding a business might look like if they were super ambitious about it. The platform also gives them access to bursaries and mentors who will support their growth aspirations.

However, while money is important when you're growing a business, I'm 100 per cent convinced that the start-ups I'm working with through the platform won't be any more successful because they've had good funding. What's far more important is information and guidance. I tell the founders I meet that if they spend as much time getting their products to market and gaining early adopters as they do securing their seed funding, they'll be more likely to succeed. That's because they'll gain early feedback from people who've actually bought their product and will keep more of the equity in their business for themselves.

Of course, the platform has to be sustainable beyond me – that much I've learned from exiting my previous business. So although I'm heavily involved in guiding the tech development at the moment, it will eventually be run by the community of business owners who use it. They'll set up events and answer questions in the forum, and the advisors and mentors will put resources into the marketplace, which will be rated by the entrepreneurs. It will be very much a self-governing environment.

I feel very blessed to choose exactly how I spend my days. My hard work and risk taking has paid off handsomely. Continuing to back myself with my own start-ups, alongside sharing my experiences to help other founders navigate their route to exit faster and less painfully than I did, and spending time with my family both in the UK and Australia is a dream come true.

I hope that by reading this book I can help you to make your entrepreneurial dreams come true too.

Quick recap

- ↗ Once you've received some bids, your next step is to attend pre-offer meetings.
- ↗ After that you decide whether to accept an offer; this triggers a presentation by your leadership team to the potential buyer and a due diligence process by them.
- ↗ It can be a shock to suddenly be outside the business you've devoted your life to, so you need to know what you're going to do next.

Questions to ask yourself

- ↗ What will I do with the money I receive when my business is sold?
- ↗ What do I want to do with my time once I'm no longer in charge?
- ↗ Is there anything I can set up now that will give me a smooth transition into a new activity after the sale?
- ↗ What are my long-term plans for the future?

Conclusion

There aren't many business owners who start a company and manage to grow it into a viable concern. In fact, only 45 per cent survive the first five years, so creating an established scale-up is a major achievement. Those who sell for a life-changing sum are exceptionally rare. So given that only a tiny minority of entrepreneurs start, scale and sell for millions, what's the secret?

There's no silver bullet of course. Instead, succeeding in business is down to getting as many decisions right, and as few wrong, as you can. One of the best ways to learn how to do this is through listening to other entrepreneurs who've been in your shoes and who've discovered their own path to success. They've been through the most effective MBA programme of all – that of the Institute of Business Failure and Success. This is why I'm indebted to the people who generously shared their experiences with me, because they've given me a rounded overview of what all entrepreneurs should know.

As I see it, these lessons break down into three main areas: the **strategic thinking** that you apply to your business; the quality of your **marketing**; and how you treat **your people and yourself**.

Every business owner must become a **strategist** if they're to scale and sell on their own terms. One of the themes throughout this book has been the importance of discovering what your market wants to buy, and then creating a product for it that has a clear point of difference. Along the way, you need to have goals and also plans for how to reach them. The added benefit of goals is that they steer you away from chasing the latest shiny new idea, a distraction that can bring down many an entrepreneur. And timing is everything, from when you launch a product right the way through to when you sell your company.

Let's turn to **marketing**. If your product is the tree that grows and bears fruit, your marketing is the fertile soil that enables it to flourish. Because if your marketing is excellent, sales will come. Great marketing starts with solving a problem better than your competitors and it's underpinned by accurate information – about both your market and your market position. Once you have that, you need to work out how to create the best marketing buzz you can afford with the money you have. And never stop making your existing customers feel appreciated and asking them what you're doing right and wrong – it's their business that will help yours to scale.

Finally, **who you are and how you treat people** are two sides of the same coin. All entrepreneurs are hard-working, optimistic and driven – they have to be. But they can't succeed on their own – they need a committed team behind them. Building a strong internal culture and trusting people to do their jobs without too much interference is something that many of us have learned the hard way. Even more challenging is looking after yourself so that you don't burn out. This can take the form of simple self-care, but also through ensuring that you carve out a role for yourself that you both enjoy and are good at. And while you're about it, don't forget to sow the seeds of another adventure for yourself after the exit.

I hope you've enjoyed coming on my entrepreneurial journey with me. If I'd known in my early days what I know now, I'd have saved myself a lot of frustration and wasted time. With this book to guide you, your venture will be based on a sound footing – practical, clear sighted and with your eyes firmly on the prize.

Just as most entrepreneurs are born rather than made, so the entrepreneurial spirit never dies. We keep reinventing ourselves through our businesses, pursuing success until it's no longer a dream. Long live entrepreneurs – may we start, scale and sell forever.

What I Learned from My MBA

My MBA taught me that there are different schools of thought about how companies grow. While writing my dissertation, I did a literature review of what the leading thinkers were saying about this subject. You may feel academic research isn't your thing and that business is more about getting out there and doing it. You'd have a point, of course. But what I've done here is to distil three years of my own research into a series of user-friendly points, all backed up with references should you want to follow them up. In effect, it's a few minutes of reading for you instead of the years I spent. I call that excellent value!

Why do firms need to grow?

This is a good question, because not every entrepreneur has an appetite for growth. At the start of 2021 there were 5.6 million private sector businesses in the UK, but only 25 per cent employed anyone other than the owner, and most of the remainder had fewer than

49 employees (BEIS 2021). What's more, fast growth is highly unusual: for every 100 start-ups, only the largest four survivors create 50 per cent of all jobs over a decade (Storey 1994, Anyadike-Danes et al. 2008, Schindele and Weyth 2011).

From the point of view of the economy, it's vital that businesses grow. It's equally important for the company itself: the survival rates of expanding businesses are twice those of ones that don't grow (Phillips and Kirchoff 1989). So if you're reading this book because you want your business to rise quickly, your ambitions are backed up by the latest research.

How businesses grow

To my mind, the most helpful research on this is by Professor David Storey of the University of Sussex. In his analysis of small business growth he identifies three key components:

↗ the characteristics of the entrepreneur at the head of the firm
↗ the characteristics of the firm
↗ the environment in which the firm trades.

It makes sense to me that these three areas (some of them under your control as a business owner, some not) make a great entry point into understanding the main factors affecting growth. Let's look at them in turn.

The entrepreneur

What does the research say about the kind of entrepreneur you'd need to be in order to grow your business super fast? To start with, leaders of firms that grow have certain attitudes in common (Massey et al. 2006). They're comfortable with delegating responsibility for operational functions so that they can focus on higher-level strategy, but this doesn't stop them from being 'hands on' in the management of their businesses, especially at the beginning (Smallbone et al. 1995). Steve Jobs and Mark Zuckerberg are examples of founders whose personalities have had a strong impact on the performance of their companies. But as time went by, they were able to loosen the reins.

Education and motivation

The educational background and qualifications of an entrepreneur can have a significant impact on his or her success. That's because the higher the education level, the more resources the founder is likely to have (Smallbone and Wyer 2000), and the higher their expectations of what they would earn (Kangasharju 2000). If their expertise lies in their business sector, such as engineering or IT, that can also give them a growth advantage (Barringer and Jones 2004). I know that people cite examples of college drop-outs like Bill Gates and Michael Dell as being exceptions to this, but they had at least got into university and were capable of completing it. It was their choice to finish early to found their companies.

Attitude to risk and previous experience

'An entrepreneurial firm is one that engages in product market innovation and understands somewhat risky adventures,' says Miller (1983). Clearly, an appetite for innovation and risk is a prerequisite for the entrepreneur. His or her previous experience also has a significant influence on the performance of the business (Singer 1995). What's more, many entrepreneurs are 'portfolio' businesspeople who are involved in several firms – these are more likely to achieve business growth (Smallbone and Wyer 2000).

Age and gender

Younger business owners are less likely to have the capital to succeed, whereas those over 55 may be looking towards retirement. This means that your age when starting a business can have an impact on its growth. Also, firms owned by men are much more likely to grow than those owned by women. This could be because female entrepreneurs have more family commitments, are possibly discriminated against or are more likely to launch their businesses in sectors with slower growth potential (Storey & Greene 2010). This isn't always the case; one of the reasons I'm writing this book is to provide a positive role model for female business owners and so change these statistics.

Size of the founding team

Most research shows that firms started by a team of entrepreneurs, as opposed to a single person, benefit from the breadth of talent, experience and resources they all bring.

The organisation

The second aspect of growing companies I looked at was the nature of the organisational set-up. What are the main characteristics of fast-growing businesses in the way that they're organised?

Resources

First of all, it makes sense that the more resources a business has, the greater its opportunities to grow. In addition, companies with access to external finance expand more rapidly than others – although there's a 'chicken and egg' possibility here because businesses which are more likely to grow are also more attractive to external investors (Becchetti & Trovato 2002). Interestingly, there's also evidence that only a limited element of a company's resources can generate sustained competitive advantage (Wade and Hulland 2004), and that these resources need to be unique to the firm in order to do so (Gottschalk 2007). That means it's not just the amount of money, time and experience your company has that's important, but the nature of it.

Product and market development

Smallbone et al. (1995) have found that the successful management of product and market development is what most consistently distinguishes high-growth businesses from others; they analysed a project which was part of the ESRC's Small Business Research Initiative, examining 306 firms between 1979 and 1990, based mainly on interviews with owner-managers. They found that to achieve consistently high growth means that businesses need to be actively interested in how their products relate to their markets. In fact, most fast-growing firms build upon an already established product base and market position, either by identifying new markets for existing products or by creating new products for existing markets at a higher value.

People and company size

The way in which business owners recruit, develop and retain their staff has an important impact on growth. Robson and Bennett (2000) show evidence of a link between employee skill levels and the growth of the firm they work in, and Storey (1994) reports that businesses which train their workforces are more likely to grow. Small, new businesses also thrive more quickly than larger, well-established ones (Evans 1987 and Hall 1987).

Flexibility

It's obviously essential for small firms to respond quickly to market changes so they can increase in size. What's less clear is whether being flexible is part of a company's culture because of the attitude of the founding entrepreneur or because it lives naturally in small companies that have grown well.

The trading environment

While the market environment is a factor influencing growth, the highest-growth firms develop an active market and product strategy to sustain them over time (Smallbone and North 1995). Small companies which have grown quickly and sustainably have always done so by differentiating themselves successfully from their competitors (Pena 2002).

Innovation

Larger corporations tend to focus on predictable, stable sales opportunities, leaving a gap in the market for riskier products and services to enter; small firms can take advantage of this. In fact, small businesses are responsible for 95 per cent of all radical innovations, often in the technology sector (Robbins et al. 2000). This has a significant impact on their growth.

Exporting

Although most small businesses don't export, exporting is an important characteristic of those with high growth (Cambridge Small Business Research Centre 1992). There may be a significant opportunity for your business here.

Industry sector

Some academics have shown that industry sector is the most critical factor in the growth of a business, more so than strategic choices and the resources available. Speaking personally, I wonder if this is true. If it is, why do investors tend to invest in the entrepreneur themself more than in the market they're planning to enter? Having said that, other thinkers say this overestimates the degree of choice a founder of a small business has about what sector they decide to enter in the first place (O'Gorman 2001).

Third party tools

Business thinkers have done a lot of the hard work for us over the years by coming up with ways of helping entrepreneurs see their business growth with fresh eyes. When I first started in business I didn't have a clue about any of these valuable resources, but through reading up on the subject and then by doing my MBA, I've discovered some incredible tools. Reacting to changes as they come along may be good enough when we're starting out, but when we're keen to grow quickly we need to stand back and do some level-headed analysis.

Models for your market

If you're like many entrepreneurs, you probably set up your business to take advantage of a gap in the market, so you know your market inside out. But what you might not be doing is monitoring it, just like it never occurred to me to monitor mine in all the years I ran Start-Right (with disastrous results at the end). Because your external environment isn't something that you can influence, let alone control, it can be easy to wonder what the point of monitoring it is. If that's your view, I hope my experience has convinced you that although you can't control it, you can still decide how you react to changes within it.

At Smart Apprentices, for instance, our market was

apprentice training providers. Any tool that helped us to audit our external environment so that we could identify upcoming political, technological and social change was of benefit to us. It meant we could create plans with two aims in mind: to mitigate risk and to take advantage of change. In fact, the most powerful thing I learned in my MBA was that changes you can't control in your external environment can transform your business for the better if you see them as opportunities before your competitors do.

This made a significant difference to us when, out of the blue, the UK government introduced legislation about how apprenticeships should be funded and assessed, leading to the creation of apprenticeship awarding organisations (AAOs). These bodies were made responsible for assessing apprentices at the end of their courses in what are called end-point assessments, which comprised a variety of methods such as interviews, observations and examinations of project work. As soon as we discovered this, we quickly scanned the market to see if there was an appetite for a new technology specifically aimed at these new AAOs. Our quick and dirty research showed us that there was a gap we could fill, so we created a brand new technology from the ground up and were first to market with it. Winning a huge customer before the development work was even finished was a boost, especially as they worked with us as a partner to improve the system. All this was as a direct result of us scanning the horizon for changes in our business environment and reacting quickly to them.

What tools and models would be helpful for you in

assessing your external business environment? You may have heard of some of these, but are you using them?

PESTLE and Porter's Five Forces

Each letter in PESTLE stands for a factor which may be changing in the industry you operate within. These are the **political, economic, social, technological, legal and environmental** aspects impacting your sector. These areas present both risks and opportunities to your business, and to assess the impact these could have, you can create a SWOT analysis of your business **(strength, weakness, opportunity and threat)**.

You can also use Porter's Five Forces model. This well-known marketing tool was developed by the marketing strategy expert Michael Porter, a professor from Harvard Business School. It's used by businesses around the world and is brilliant for helping you analyse where the power lies in a business situation. By looking at the relative leverage of your suppliers, competitors and customers, you can spot threats and opportunities which you wouldn't otherwise have known existed (Porter 2008).

Models for your business

PESTLE and Porter's Five Forces are indispensable in helping you to analyse your external environment, along with your fitness to thrive in it. But what about looking more inwardly at your business? You have your people, financial set-up, product development, marketing and other factors to juggle. How do you know if you're well balanced across these areas? If you're not able to access finance, for instance, this will impact on your product development and therefore on your ability to take advantage of opportunities in your marketplace.

My own balanced inward-focused business model

I created my own way of checking our internal business balance. Here's a diagram of how it works:

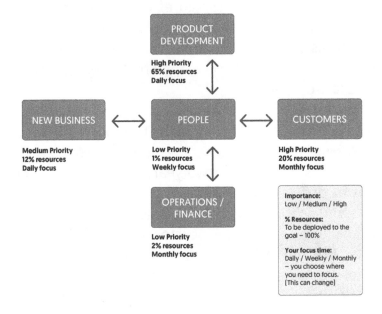

*Smart Apprentices' inward-focused business model,
with figures for 2017*

To use this helpful model for yourself, divide your business into each of these five key areas: product development, new business, people, customers and operations/finance. Ask yourself the following questions about each one:

1. How important is delivering our business strategy in this area this year? High, medium, or low (H/M/L)?
2. What percentage of our available resources (people, time and money) do we currently deploy towards achieving this?
3. How much time do I personally spend on this area on a daily, weekly and monthly basis (D/W/M)?

I've used my business figures to bring the model to life, but you can add your own data to make it relevant to you. As an example, here's what the model reveals regarding our product development during one year of our scale-up phase.

Delivering our business strategy in product development in 2017 was of high importance to us; otherwise we risked not achieving our revenue growth predictions for the next two years. At the time, 65 per cent of our resources were invested in achieving this goal, and as this aspect of our business was one of our two highest priorities (our customers being the other), it felt like the right balance. I spent time most days reviewing, supporting and inputting into our product development, which was appropriate because I had the skills to shape and influence both the functionality and the look and feel of our new products.

However, as our new products were released to market throughout 2017, the importance of product development would decrease from high to medium. My time would also decrease along with it, while the importance of new business would move to high, along with increased resources to match and the amount of time I'd spend on that area.

The truth about fast-growing businesses

When I did my MBA my task was not only to wade through a huge amount of expert literature, illuminating though that was. I also did my own research because I wanted to talk to living, breathing entrepreneurs who had a proven record of growing their companies super fast. So I interviewed a selection of business owners who'd made it into the *Sunday Times* Tech Track 100 list. The companies on this list are Britain's fastest-growing technology companies, with a sales growth from at least £250,000 in the year from when their sales were measured to at least £5 million in the most recent year. Here I summarise what I found so that you can assess both yourself and your business against them. You might be surprised at what you discover.

The secret ingredients for success

What did I learn to be the common characteristics of fast-growth entrepreneurs? They're male, under 40, have used their own assets as start-up capital, are educated to at least degree level, have had a previous business failure and have started up with at least one business partner. Most interestingly, they identify their key motivation for starting their businesses as the need to prove they can succeed (I can certainly relate to that).

Let's move on to their people. Their management team members are shareholders, are educated to at least degree level and have a strong desire to grow the company. They ensure that the business keeps adapting and changing its product range, actively seek new markets and have an action-oriented mindset.

Finally, what's the typical nature of the fast-growth

company's operating environment? In my conversations with the owners, I found this to be a lesser influence than the other factors. Most businesses operated in a competitive market with more than ten key competitors, but this gave them the opportunity to find gaps in the market and fill them quickly by solving customer problems better than anyone else.

How do these characteristics relate to you? There's nothing to say you have to fit an identikit of the 'ideal entrepreneur' – I'm hardly one myself in every respect, being female and in my late 50s when I sold Smart Apprentices. But in some of the areas that differed from my own, I found inspiration and ideas that helped me to grow.

To end with, you'll be interested to see a representative selection of the answers I was given when I asked my interviewees this question: 'What do you think has contributed to your company growing so quickly?' Here they are:

↗ 'Going to market with something different.'
↗ 'Wanting to grow.'
↗ 'Lots of tenacity, especially when times are tough.'
↗ 'Some luck, but I guess the harder you work the luckier you get.'
↗ 'Working in partnership with our clients.'
↗ 'Thought leadership – showing our customers we're the experts.'
↗ 'Finding the curve – seeing what's about to change and how we could bring something to market ahead of that change.'
↗ 'We brought products to market quickly, before they were ready, then figured out what we had to

do to make them work with our customers.'
- ↗ 'Staying niche and focusing on doing it well.'
- ↗ 'Driving transformation, not just selling technology.'
- ↗ 'Being aggressive and hungry, wanting the growth, being ambitious.'
- ↗ 'Moving quickly, not hesitating.'
- ↗ 'Building strategic relationships with the most senior people in our client base.'
- ↗ 'Fear of failure, and also having something to prove, led me to relentlessly grow this business.'

Do any of these ring a bell? You may be even more interested to read a selection of answers to this question: 'What would you do differently if you had your time again?' After all, we'd love to have a crystal ball, wouldn't we?

- ↗ 'Never run out of cash.'
- ↗ 'Stand back from the detail on a regular basis – it's hard to let go of it.'
- ↗ 'Pace myself and my team. I learned that building a business is like running a marathon, but it's best to do it in a series of sprints and recover in between.'
- ↗ 'Be more ruthless on the people side – I think I may have been too tolerant when I should have made changes.'
- ↗ 'Start my company at a younger age.'
- ↗ 'Go for global reach when still a small company.'
- ↗ 'Invest more of my own money initially to keep more equity – I wish I hadn't been scared to remortgage or sell the house.'
- ↗ 'Start earlier, take more risks.'
- ↗ 'Better exit planning from the start.'

↗ 'Create a more streamlined corporate structure with better funding.'

↗ 'Find a problem and solve it better than anyone else.'

↗ 'Having achieved huge growth in the first two years, we stagnated because we lost our hunger for growth. We should have kept up the pace.'

↗ 'Nothing. Every decision, success and mistake has taught us invaluable lessons.'

What can you take from these models, answers and research? And what will you do differently from now on?

References

Anyadike-Danes, M., Bonner, K., Hart, M. & Symington, D. (2008) *Escaping the Dead Hand of the Past: The direct employment effects of new firm formation and the dynamics of job growth in Northern Ireland 1995–2005.* Economic Research Institute of Northern Ireland.

Barringer, B.R. & Jones, F.F. (2004) 'Achieving rapid growth – revisiting the managerial capacity problem'. *Journal of Development Entrepreneurship* 9(1).

Becchetti, L. & Trovato, G. (2002) 'The determinants of growth for small and medium sized firm: The role of the availability of external finance'. *Small Business Economics* 19(4).

BEIS (2021) 'Business population estimates for the UK and regions 2021: statistical release'. URL: gov.uk/government/statistics/business-population-estimates-2021/business-population-estimates-for-the-uk-and-regions-2021-statistical-release-html

Cambridge Small Business Research Centre (1992) *The State of British Enterprises.* Department of Applied Economics, University of Cambridge.

Evans, D. (1987) 'Tests of alternative theories of firm growth.' *The Journal of Political Economy* 95(4).

Gottschalk, P. (2007) *Business Dynamics in Information Technology.* Ideas Group Inc.

Hall, B.H. (1987) 'The relationship between firm size and firm growth in the US manufacturing sector'. *Journal of Industrial Economics* 35(4).

Kangasharju, A. (2000) 'Growth of the smallest: determinants of small firm growth during strong macroeconomic fluctuations'. *International Small Business Journal* 19(1).

Miller, D. (1983) 'The correlates of entrepreneurship in three types of firms'. *Management Science* 29(7).

O'Gorman, C. (2001) 'The sustainability of growth in small and medium sized enterprises'. *International Journal of Entrepreneurial Behaviour & Research* 7(2).

Pena, I. (2002) 'Intellectual capital and business start-up success'. *Journal of Intellectual Capital* 3(2).

Phillips, B. & Kirchoff, B. (1989) 'Formation, growth and survival: small firm dynamics in the US economy'. *Small Business Economics* 1(1).

Porter, M.E. (2008) 'The Five Competitive Forces That Shape Strategy'. *Harvard Business Review*, January 2008. URL: hbr.org/2008/01/the-five-competitive-forces-that-shape-strategy

Robbins, D.K., Pantuosco, L.J., Parker, D.F., Fuller, B.K. (2000) 'An empirical assessment of the contribution of small business employment to US state economic performance'. *Small Business Economics* 15(4).

Robson, P.J.A. & Bennett, R.J. (2000) 'SME growth: the relationship with business advice and external collaboration'. *Small Business Economics* 15(3).

Schindele, Y. & Weyth, A. (2011) 'The direct employment effects of new business in Germany revisited: an empirical investigation for 1976-2004'. *Small Business Economics* 36(3).

Smallbone, D., Leigh, R. & North, D. (1995) 'The characteristics and strategies of high growth SMEs'. *International Journal of Entrepreneurial Behaviour & Research* 1(3).

Smallbone, D. & Wyer, P. (2000) 'Growth and development in the small firm' in Carter, S. & James-Evans, D. (eds). *Enterprise and Small Business*. Prentice Hall.

Storey, D.J. (1994) *Understanding the Small Business Sector*. Routledge.

Storey, D.J. & Greene, F.J. (2010) *Small Business and Entrepreneurship*. Financial Times/Prentice Hall/Pearson.

Wade, M. & Hulland, J. (2004) 'Review: The resource-based view and information systems research: review, extension and suggestions for future research'. *MIS Quarterly* 28(1).

Acknowledgements

I would like to thank my four children, Richard, Bradey, Emma and Saoirse for their unwavering support, belief and love. They have been my inspiration for achieving greatness and love me just the way I am.

Thank you to Ginny Carter for patiently listening to my story and telling it so eloquently in this book.

I would like to thank fellow Helm members Tom Carroll, Chris Morling, Rob Hamilton, Alison Cooper, Chris Cole, Varun Gupta and Ian Cassidy for so candidly telling their stories. Helm is a supporting community of scale-up founders which the contributors and author belong to.

Also the wonderful team I had around me at Smart Apprentices: Andy, Ann, Danny, Helen, Hilary, Lisa, Marcus and Mark, who were steadfast in their confidence and support in my leadership.

The Author

Fiona Hudson-Kelly is one of Britain's most successful female technology entrepreneurs.

Aged 26, she set up a computer training company and quickly attracted large clients such as the Rover Group. However, her world turned upside down when her biggest client unexpectedly collapsed overnight. She lost her entire business in just a few days, and at the same time became a single mother to four children; emotionally and financially she was running on empty.

Against the odds, Fiona started a new technology company which sold for millions in 2016. Not content with one successful exit, she went on to found her second technology company, Smart Apprentices, which she sold in 2021 – also for a multi-million-pound sum.

Never one to sit still, Fiona has recently launched an innovative and disruptive recruitment technology platform. It's inspired by her frustrations, as a fast-growing employer, with recruiting and retaining great talent. The platform's unbiased and vibrant ecosystem helps employers to find highly skilled people who also fit their team dynamics.

Fiona's goal is to achieve a hat-trick of successful exits. In the meantime, she shares her knowledge and experience through speaking and also her evolving platform for entrepreneurs. Her goal is to help everyone who's interested in starting a business, especially women and girls, to be more ambitious in their entrepreneurial endeavours and to consider rapidly scaling and selling their businesses for many millions.

If you'd like to hear Fiona speak on your stage, inspiring your audience to be more ambitious and to create their own wealth and independence from nothing, please visit **www.fionahudsonkelly.com**.